A PRACTICAL GUIDE TO USING STORYLINE ACROSS THE CURRICULUM

A Practical Guide to Using Storyline Across the Curriculum **provides a comprehensive introduction to the Storyline approach to teaching and learning – an approach that embraces and encourages children's passion for learning. Putting children at the centre of learning, the book explores how educators and teachers can harness pupils' innate appetite for stories to make interdisciplinary teaching and learning enjoyable and successful.**

Demonstrating how teachers can easily use the Storyline approach within the curriculum, this book offers a step-by-step introduction to learning developed through the use of narrative. Key topics explained include:

- planning individual lessons and sequences of lessons;
- guidance on planning and progress;
- assessment and evaluation of learning;
- links with visible learning and growth mindset approaches.

Filled with detailed examples of storylines that have been tried and tested in the classroom, *A Practical Guide to Using Storyline Across the Curriculum* offers new and experienced teachers an accessible guide to the Storyline approach, with ready-to-use ideas to enable, inspire and support learners.

Peter Tarrant has been involved in teaching for 36 years and is a Senior Teaching Fellow in Initial Teacher Education at the University of Edinburgh, UK. He has been involved in a number of research projects involving topics such as teacher confidence and behaviour management, developing reflective practice and using a peer learning approach towards metacognitive practice. He is author of *Metacognition in the Primary Classroom* (Routledge 2015). Peter regularly does INSET in schools and colleges and can be contacted at ptarrant9@gmail.com.

A PRACTICAL GUIDE TO USING STORYLINE ACROSS THE CURRICULUM

Inspiring Learning with Passion

Peter Tarrant

LONDON AND NEW YORK

First published 2019
by Routledge
2 Park Square, Milton Park, Abingdon, Oxon OX14 4RN

and by Routledge
711 Third Avenue, New York, NY 10017

Routledge is an imprint of the Taylor & Francis Group, an informa business

© 2019 Peter Tarrant

The right of Peter Tarrant to be identified as author of this work has been asserted by him in accordance with sections 77 and 78 of the Copyright, Designs and Patents Act 1988.

All rights reserved. No part of this book may be reprinted or reproduced or utilised in any form or by any electronic, mechanical, or other means, now known or hereafter invented, including photocopying and recording, or in any information storage or retrieval system, without permission in writing from the publishers.

Trademark notice: Product or corporate names may be trademarks or registered trademarks, and are used only for identification and explanation without intent to infringe.

British Library Cataloguing in Publication Data
A catalogue record for this book is available from the British Library

Library of Congress Cataloging in Publication Data
A catalog record has been requested for this book

ISBN: 978-1-138-48316-3 (hbk)
ISBN: 978-1-138-48317-0 (pbk)
ISBN: 978-1-351-05566-6 (ebk)

Typeset in Interstate
by Swales & Willis Ltd, Exeter, Devon, UK

Visit the eResources: www.routledge.com/9781138483170

Printed and bound by CPI Group (UK) Ltd, Croydon, CR0 4YY

This book is dedicated to Steve Bell, Sallie Harkness and Fred Rendell, the ones with the wisdom and creativity to start Storyline in the 1960s.

To Barbara Frame, who passed the mantle on to me.

And to thousands of student teachers who allowed me to enthuse and inspire them to try it too.

I do hope that this book will open a door for those creative enough to look inside.

Peter Tarrant

CONTENTS

Acknowledgements ix

Part I: The theory, philosophy and approach explained 1

   Introduction 3

1. What is Storyline? 5
2. Learning and the curriculum 12
3. Learning and pedagogy 23
4. What does Storyline look like in the classroom? 34

Part II: Four approaches to planning a storyline 39

5. The Street: a WWII storyline, plan and process 41
6. The Letter: *The Owl Who Was Afraid of the Dark* and a Health and Wellbeing storyline 52
7. The Challenge: *Junior Dragons' Den* and *The Apprentice* storylines 66
8. The Visitor: A Visitor from Space, *The Lighthouse Keeper's Lunch* and a Rabbie Burns storyline 71

Part III: Assessment and planning approaches 79

9. Choosing your Storyline approach 81
10. Storyline and curriculum planning 92
11. Ways of presenting and assessing the learning 100

Part IV: Appendices – practitioner examples, plans, case studies and templates 109

1. Storyline in a day 111
2. Alien writing frame 117

3	Practitioner example: Alien Story	119
4	Practitioner example: WWII plan	121
5	Practitioner example: Highland Clearances (the Street)	127
6	Practitioner example: Wizard School (the Street)	133
7	Practitioner example: Mary Queen of Scots	137
8	Practitioner example: Forest School (the Letter)	140
9	Practitioner example: Our Railway	145
10	Practitioner example: The Middle Ages (the Challenge)	147
11	Practitioner example: Egypt	149
12	Practitioner example: Wind Farm	152
13	Practitioner example: New Neighbours and Refugees (the Street)	156
14	Synopsis planning pro forma	163
15	Storyline planning pro forma	165
16	Storyline planning template	166
17	WWII complete synopsis	168
18	WWII complete plan	169
19	Rainforest complete synopsis	172
20	Rainforest complete plan	174
21	Deforestation example	177
22	Assessment pro forma	181
23	Completed assessment grid	183
24	Using templates	185
	Index	190

ACKNOWLEDGEMENTS

I would like to give special thanks to those listed below.

These brave souls aided me in my research by trialling different kinds of storylines, many of which are featured in this book.

Given just a brief introduction and little support, these students and teachers creatively embraced the Storyline principles and ran with the approach.

It is teachers like these that enrich our current education system.

Jenny Bayliss
Jo Briggs
Beth Christie
Sarah Clark
Jane Coatham
Belinda Cook
Lisa Cosgrove
Stephanie Cowan
Louise Ferguson
Daryl Gladstone
Elaine Hastings
Kathryn Ireland
Anni Mackay
Erin Murray
Linda Murray
PGDE students 2016-2017
Kirsteen Ramsay

Staff and pupils at Bonnyrigg Primary School

Annie Stockdale
Stephanie Waugh
Jacqueline Wilkinson

Part I
The theory, philosophy and approach explained

Introduction

Learning with passion

Learning with passion. This part of the title of this book may have attracted you because that's what you feel about learning and teaching.

Sometimes it is reassuring to read that you are not alone in your views, values and beliefs.

Whether you are a teacher or not, you probably already know the buzz to be had from enabling, inspiring and supporting learners who are excited to learn. This passion for learning is priceless and perhaps our role as educators is to somehow kindle that spark, feed that fire and support that passion until it enables the learner to flourish. Clearly not everyone will be that performer, that joker or tale teller that is loved by all children and who seems to inspire passion effortlessly.

However, we can take comfort in the fact that we have all experienced a wide range of personalities of different teachers in different settings. They were all different but each had the capacity to light that fuse of passion for us. What these people had in common, perhaps, was a love of learning itself and the confidence and enthusiasm to pass that on to us.

This book explores how a Storyline approach might equip the teacher or leader to share and generate that passion for learning. The approach is steeped in curiosity and community.

It provides inspiration, consternation and jubilation, as a problem is solved or a person in need is rescued. The Storyline approach uses a narrative as a framework that provides a clear plan for learning together with the security that the learners can have ownership of their own learning.

Regardless of our own teaching experience and abilities we will always struggle if the learner is unwilling to co-operate. Indeed, many teachers thrive on the response of the pupils in order to properly express themselves in the classroom. For some this relationship is like that of the actor live on stage, reaching out to their audience and then feeding off the reaction. In teaching this might manifest itself as the things that the teacher says and does to motivate, inspire and intrigue the learners in their care. There is a kind of magic when the relationship is strong and the learners 'believe' in the teacher. This sense of trust is what provides the right climate for learning to flourish.

Taking a narrative approach to teaching and learning enables those participating to experience an emotional relationship with the learning. Having the pupils 'become' families existing in the midst of World War II (WWII) means that they have a memorable experience – an experience in which they actually care about the events and scenarios. It means that they have that vital ingredient for independent learning: the gift of curiosity.

In my experience, learners involved in this approach are generally keen and passionate about their characters or creations. They want to have 'another episode,' another chapter of a story where they find out more and more of the puzzle. One where they can have an influence or impact on what unravels.

Of course, much depends on trust, relationships and the teachers' ability to 'weave the magic spell.' The learners need to believe in the project – to willingly suspend their disbelief sufficiently to play their part in the fiction. When they come into the classroom and see the crashed rocket with a letter from the alien, they know that this is a game of pretend, yet they readily embrace the fantasy and are desperate to carry out the research on behalf of their new alien friend. They will go away and learn all about the Earth or the planets – motivated by the desire to 'play the game.' This is where the passion and enthusiasm comes from. It thrives on a sense of community and joint enterprise. The learners want to support and help the (fictional) character.

For the teacher this provides many opportunities for learning 'about' (people, places, things) and puts the learning 'in a context' (engaging in a fantasy where we all accept that we can only do certain things because of the time and place where the story takes place – no, we can't use our smartphones because this is World War II!).

It is such a powerful experience when this learning with passion happens. It is not just the enthusiasm of the teacher. It is the desire in the learners to find out, to share and to communicate. Pupils encourage each other and the collaborative group effort in turn develops and builds an ethos of enquiry and support, and a community of learners.

When we think back to things we have learned ourselves it is often those experiences that go together with a sense of adventure, a sense of community and of joint endeavour that we remember best. Learning in and through experience must be one of the most enjoyable, rewarding and memorable ways to learn – hence the current emphasis in education on learning through 'play,' and on outdoor learning. What this book attempts to do is to give teachers the scope to take their pupils to places, times and experiences that would be impossible in real life – but extremely accessible through the shared narrative of a storyline.

Learning with passion is something to feel very passionate about!

1 What is Storyline?

This book is all about the Storyline approach to teaching and learning. It is a pedagogy and a methodology that puts the child at the centre of learning. It looks to the child to stimulate and follow their passion and interest to learn. It acknowledges what the child already knows, and treasures their curiosity to find out more.

At first sight you might ask, "Where is there the freedom to do all of this in a climate with an already overcrowded curriculum and so many demands for assessment and attainment?"

This book hopes to convince you that not only is it possible to enjoy Storyline and serve these different 'masters,' but that it will be an extremely effective, and most of all fun, way to do it.

So what is Storyline?

Human beings are hard-wired to make connections, to look for patterns and to construct a narrative in order to make sense of the world and their surroundings.

For example, look at these words then close your eyes and think about them:

> island   sand   sinking   man   safety   treasure   swam

The chances are that you linked some of these together and began to construct a narrative – something like this:

> The boat sank and the man swam to the island for safety. Later he found treasure.

The point is, we are conditioned to try to make sense of things. Given even a random mix of information, words or stimuli, our brains are programmed to look for patterns and connections. A primal form of this is the construction of a narrative. Through stories we can make sense of the world. We can make information relatable and see how it fits our own schemas and experiences.

The more relatable the story the more memorable it will be. If we invest some feelings and emotions into the story it will also help our memory and our understanding.

When you think about learning you often recall a person or emotion that is connected: perhaps your favourite teacher, or some learning experiences that you recall as being fun.

Storyline taps into this innate desire for a narrative. It encourages participants to construct a narrative and adopt ownership. It is connected with emotions: the most common adjectives used by participants to describe the experience are words like *enthusiastic*, *passionate*, *motivated*, *engrossed* and, of course, *fun*.

A classroom full of children engaged in a storyline is one where there is much talk, laughter and collaboration and the buzz of a shared adventure.

Storyline comes in many forms but one of the most common structures involves a story with a family at the heart of the narrative.

The learners create their own families and begin, right from the start, to identify with one or two of the characters. Although the learners create and develop these characters it is within the parameters laid down by the teacher, i.e. the teacher will decide where and when the family exists, they will decide on what happens to them. Meanwhile the learners will decide what the characters are like and how they will react to the events that unfold as revealed by the teacher.

To be consistent with this notion of the narrative, the following passage presents the narrative of a typical storyline which is based on a template (see Chapter 5) called the Street.

Most storylines are based on a series of 'episodes.'

1. Context
2. Families
3. Homes
4. Everyday life
5. An incident
6. Response
7. Celebration
8. Plenary

Below we can look at an example of how this might look in the classroom.

---

1 Context

Teacher:

"Today we are going to begin our topic and so the first thing we are going to do is to imagine we have travelled in a time machine. We have travelled back in time to a place up in the Scottish Highlands. We have travelled a long time back, over 150 years back in time."

2 Families

Teacher:

"What do you think people looked like then? What did they wear? What did they do for work and leisure? If you don't know, how could we find out?"

"In your groups [of 4-6 pupils] you are going to be a family in this time and place long ago. Have a chat about who you are going to be. Each person must be a member of the family. Each family group will need a family or clan name. Decide who you are and what you are like, and think about what kind of person you are - who do you get on with? Who don't you get on with? What are you good at, and so on."

After five or six minutes:
Teacher:

"Now we are going to make our characters. You will be given simple templates to draw around. You can choose male, female or child. You can then use the scrap materials to 'dress' the characters. Be creative, use as much detail as you can.

"Once your character is ready we will put each family member on to a family group portrait. The portraits will be hung on our display and then each person will be introduced to the class."

(continued)

8 *The theory, philosophy and approach*

(continued)

Once this is done, the pupils will have the opportunity to write a biography of their character. This can be a description, an annotated picture, a fact file or any other form of presentation with which the class are familiar.

The script above is taken from a Storyline topic called 'Long Ago in Scotland,' which I worked on many years ago with Sallie Harkness. She has worked on Storyline for almost 50 years with primary, high school and further education pupils, as well as adult learners in education, industry and services like the NHS and the police.

3 Homes

It is important to think through how these will be displayed. In this script the homes would be pinned up on a frieze. On other occasions they could be made from cereal boxes to create a 3D street. Sometimes they could be done with shoeboxes to create a 3D model.

The main thing to think about is the relative size of each home. To this end it is important to give approximate dimensions – or templates – to ensure that each home is in proportion to those around it.

The script would continue with the pupils developing 'homes' for their families.

In the classroom there would be a display that grows with the topic. At first it would have the families and perhaps a biography or fact file for each character. Then the homes would be added. After that the pupils can really take ownership with ideas about how each character interacts with others in that community and with their environment expressed through imaginative writing, drama and art.

(continued)

(continued)

4 Everyday life

It is clear to see here how interesting and exciting this will be for the pupils. They develop the characters and the story. Meanwhile the teacher holds the line. The teacher decides the 'where and when' of the story. In this episode the class will be asked to think about what life might have been like for families like theirs. At this point some background information might be required. This can be provided by the teacher with books, resources and web links, or this can be a research-and-present task where pupils find out what they can about living in this time and place.

5 An incident

Once the pupils have explored 'ordinary daily life,' the teacher will introduce a problem or conflict to be resolved. It may be that new neighbours arrive and have an impact on the community (see the examples in this book regarding storylines called 'WWII' in Appendix 4 and 'New Neighbours' in Appendix 13). It may be that there is a threat to be resolved, as in a topic such as 'the Vikings' and 'the Romans.' Or it might be a natural hazard or disaster, as in a topic like 'the Rainforest,' 'the Great Flood,' or 'Earthquakes.'

6 Response

Once the teacher introduces this 'jeopardy,' this drives the narrative into a sphere where the pupils are encouraged to find out more information. They are obliged to collaborate and work together. They will need to think creatively and problem solve. They may need to test a hypothesis or debate and negotiate a solution to the problem. It is through these responses that the real learning is derived – not just in terms of skills and knowledge, but also in terms of attitudes and interpersonal skills.

Of course, as it is the teacher who holds the line it is the teacher who has already planned the ways in which the conflict or jeopardy might drive the learning.

With the teacher having already considered the learning required through curriculum guidelines and the way that the storyline might provide for some of that learning to be explored and used in context, the pupils can enjoy the feeling of an exploration controlled by them whilst the teacher is secure in the knowledge that along the way they will pick up the skills and knowledge required and begin to learn how life is not separated into many disciplines but is in fact an interdisciplinary quest to find answers and solutions.

7 Celebration

It is important to have an end-point in mind when planning a storyline (otherwise they can literally go on for ever!). A solution to the problem, a successful resolution or a celebration is a good way to end. This is where much of the summative assessment can be made with each family sharing in some way the things that they have learned through participation in the topic. This might be a PowerPoint presentation, a drama or a series of articles or pieces of writing. It might take the form of a 'museum' set up to share with other pupils and their parents.

8 Plenary

The last episode is one of the most important. This is where the teacher guides the pupils to realise just how much learning has taken place. This metacognition is crucial if they are to understand and value the less obvious learning that has taken place.

For example, their:

- ability to work well with others, to negotiate and compromise;
- developing attitudes towards the content of the topic;
- mindset and learning dispositions, like resilience and determination;
- knowledge about the topic itself;
- skills in listening, talking, reading, writing, researching and presenting, etc.

You can see from the above that Storyline is a very valuable tool for implementing the curriculum in interesting and creative ways. However, in most educational establishments teachers have an obligation to work within curriculum guidelines set out by the local authority or government. Many of the authorities also have a lot of influence over not only what is to be taught, but also how it is to be taught.

In the next two chapters we will investigate some of the factors that influence what is taught and how it is taught in the primary school. The aim would be to consider where a Storyline approach might support the implementation of both content and methodology and provide something both worthwhile and powerful at the same time.

Even in the most prescriptive curriculum there is potential for the use of this Storyline pedagogy to deliver the required learning. This book aims to demonstrate how you might do what your government or local authority requires in terms of the curriculum whilst sharing the passion for learning in an interdisciplinary way. Learning like this enables different areas of the curriculum to be explored simultaneously and in a meaningful context. The narrative should provide an opportunity for rich learning in terms of knowledge, skills, concepts and attitudes.

Storyline also provides opportunities to include things like Formative Assessment (Shirley Clarke), Metacognition (Tarrant and Holt), Mindset (Carol Dweck) and Visible Learning (John Hattie) to be used as a way to promote lifelong learning attitudes and skills.

Summary

In this chapter we have grappled with a definition for Storyline and outlined its key principles and approaches. We have explored one Storyline approach based on the concept of a 'family,' in a narrative where pupils are invited to 'become' the characters living in a particular time and place and experiencing what life was like in that context.

Links between Storyline and other pedagogies like Visible Learning, Formative Assessment and Metacognition were also explored.

2 Learning and the curriculum

In this chapter we will consider what is meant when we talk about learning. This will be helpful when we consider Storyline approaches and the quest to improve the effectiveness and enjoyment of the learning process. We then look at a brief history of the curriculum in England and Scotland and consider how the way that learning has been organised has changed over the decades.

'What is learning?' 'How do we learn?'

When you consider these questions there are a number of possible responses:

- Imitation:
    - learning by copying/imitating - young children do this when they formulate their first words.
- Responding:
    - learning in response to stimuli: for example, the senses - learning about smells and tastes we like and therefore being attracted to them; not eating your greens, for example. This might be linked to conditioned responses (Skinner's pigeons, etc.).
- Rewards:
    - learning through reward - behaviourism, for example; learning to be quiet in order to be first out to break time (extrinsic motivation).
- Interest:
    - learning through interest (intrinsic motivation). Children might be motivated by dinosaurs/soldiers/trains/spaceships and explosions.
- Ambition:
    - learning through ambition - needing to learn how to drive so you can become a bus driver, or how to pass your exams in order to go to university.

What is learning anyway?

In order to grapple with this question, it is useful to consider some of the useful terms often used in association with learning:

Pedagogy	How we learn approaches, structures and processes
Epistemology	Ways of knowing/understanding
Disciplines	Disciplines should be seen as 'modes of enquiry' and not as subjects, according to David Carr
Subjects	Curricular areas such as Maths, English and History
Curriculum	Made up of subjects
Learning	Knowing something, being able to do something, making connections, improving

Pedagogy

Pedagogy is all about how we enable the learning to take place.

We can be direct and didactic – telling the learners what to do. This is efficient and sometimes effective. It was used for centuries all over the world and still exists in many universities. However, it rarely actually 'involves' the learner. It doesn't afford them much autonomy or ownership of the learning. The learner is a consumer in a situation where someone (the teacher) is promoting something (an idea or set of information) for them to consume.

Alternatively, we can be more inclusive. We can consider the interests and abilities of the learner. We can involve them actively in the learning process. We can also allow them some responsibility in terms of what they learn and how they learn this. This is closer to the way that modern primary schools are organised. The pedagogies employed involve problem-solving and group work. It might include co-operative working and teamwork. Generally, it is a pedagogy that enables the child to be fully involved and for the teacher to no longer be the 'sage on the stage,' but instead to be the 'guide from the side.'

Pedagogy, then, is all about how the learning is shared with the learner – it can be delivered or it can be something that the learner is invited to partake in.

Of course, these examples are the extremes and most schools employ a range of approaches from somewhere between these two points.

Epistemology

Within the learning approaches there are some things that require different approaches. Some areas of learning have different ways of thinking, different ways of knowing. For example, organising ideas and information in Maths and Physics may be different from organising ideas for Art or Music. If the thinking is different, then in terms of the curriculum perhaps the teaching has to be different too. Hence the traditional approach towards the curriculum where each subject had its distinct place. Maths was different from Science, and both were different from Music and Literacy. Separate ways of knowing demanded different ways of teaching and learning. This belief provided the backbone to the way the curriculum was, and still is, organised into different disciplines and subjects.

Disciplines

Disciplines are not the same as subjects. As mentioned above, some learning is based on the epistemology – different ways of knowing. For example, as a subject Science might be characterised by a few 'disciplines – or ways of working' or 'modes of enquiry':

- making a hypothesis and testing it out;
- taking systematic measurements and looking for patterns;
- repeating the patterns and then generalising into a law;
- creating simplified models to help explain phenomena;
- probing the natural world by using 'what happens if . . .' investigations;
- explaining phenomena using existing theories.

So, when thinking about learning it might be helpful to think about what there is about it that is 'unique.' In what way might seeing, doing, exploring and proving look different in, for example, Maths and Language, or Art and History?

The traditional way that curriculums are organised is to divide learning into neat categories: Maths, Language, Biology, Physics, Drama, Art, etc.

For many, many years one complaint in high schools was that different departments did not 'speak to each other.' The connections between learning in different areas were not made explicit. Transferrable learning was never acknowledged.

At this point it is interesting to consider the traditional way that learning is set out.

Traditional learning pathways

Early Years

First we learn about everything. Learning is messy; it crosses all disciplinary boundaries and is not confined in any way. The way that the learning happens involves a variety of approaches and techniques; developing thinking is a problem-solving challenge with no boundaries or rules. The child learns what they want – mostly through trial and error and discovery.

In pre-school, nursery, and Early Years this includes something called 'Learning through Play' or 'Active Learning.'

Middle primary

Next comes a more formal approach to learning. Instead of the self-motivated approach to learning where we learn 'what we need to know' in answer to interest and curiosity, we now experience a more systematic 'curricular learning.' This might involve literacy, numeracy, etc., in the classroom – often divided up into subjects and sequences of lessons. Maths is different from Science and Music different from Drama, for example. The formalisation of the curriculum has begun. On one hand critics argue this means that learners can achieve a depth of knowledge and skills in each discipline. On the other hand, critics argue that the subjects are too separate and many learners struggle to see the connections between what they learn in each of the separate subjects.

Upper primary

As we progress through primary school we learn more and more about different curricular areas, or disciplines. With each discipline come different approaches and definitions of knowledge, skills, understanding and capacities.

High school

Post primary school, traditionally, we focus in more depth on different subjects and disciplines. We are encouraged to select and narrow our options until we think in terms of Languages, Sciences, Expressive Arts, Mathematics, all 'disciplines' in their own right. The requirement to sit and pass exams further narrows the curriculum. There is a syllabus to be taught – inevitably it becomes less about what the learner wants to learn and more about what the teacher has to teach.

University

At university we continue to focus even more precisely, narrowing our aim on one or two disciplines. Depending on which degree you do, the curriculum will be either very prescriptive or very creative.

Life?

Once in the world of employment we may, or may not, remain within this narrow sphere of learning and understanding.

Yet in real life learning and knowing do not sit in separate subject areas. In life learning is messy and complicated. Things interconnect and overlap. The person directing a ballet isn't stuck in dance or music or drama, but instead mixing these with a bit of maths, biology and art.

The person installing the central heating has to know about shape, pattern, pressure, measure, literacy, etc.

In real life having single-subject knowledge entirely divorced from everything else just would not work.

So when we think about learning and pedagogy and curriculum we need to think about why we are learning. Yes, there are arguments for learning a discipline for its own sake, but to survive and thrive in real life we need to enable the learners to be independent and to make connections. Later on in the book I hope to show how an interdisciplinary approach like Storyline helps to develop the ability to make connections and to progress transferrable learning from a very early age.

A brief history of the curriculum: organised learning in the UK since the 1950s

Up to the 1950s in many UK schools

- The curriculum in primary school was clearly defined. The teacher's role was to teach a list of content (facts).
- For each subject there was a textbook.
- The process (or methodology) was not considered important – learning was mainly by rote practice and memorising.

During the 1960s

'Primary Education in Scotland 1965' (the Primary Memorandum)

During the 1960s education became more 'progressive,' with lots of new theories, ideas and ways of organising schools, from new approaches to the teaching of reading to open-plan architecture. There was a move towards a less formal curriculum and more of a focus on child-centred education and an emphasis on learning through discovery.

In Scotland 'Primary Education in Scotland 1965' set out new approaches towards the curriculum.

It attempted to implement a child-centred and holistic approach to teaching where there was less emphasis on textbooks and distinct curricular areas. Instead it advocated learning through play and discovery. It organised many subjects into integrated areas for thematic study; for example, instead of History, Geography and Nature Studies an integrated topic or Environmental Studies was introduced.

This new curriculum for primary schools in Scotland reorganised some subjects into areas of study – for example:

- language arts (reading, writing, speaking, listening);
- environmental studies (history, geography, science, etc.);
- aesthetic subjects (art, music, drama and movement).

– and recommended a much more holistic approach. This meant thinking of processes and strategies (methodologies) as opposed to focusing on learning content and information.

This approach was termed 'thematic' or 'interdisciplinary.' It involved teachers encouraging learners to make connections and to see how learning was linked and integrated. At this time many teachers planned their projects with the topic in the middle of the page with all of the curricular areas around it. They would then think of lessons they could do to develop all aspects of the topic.

Although this did enable learners to make connections and to experience transferrable learning, one of the criticisms was that the learning could often become contrived and superficial.

It was during this period that the Storyline approach was born.

1967: the Plowden Report

Meanwhile, two years later the Plowden Report also moved the curriculum in England along in a similarly progressive direction. This period in curriculum history was one of great freedom and creativity for teacher and pupil. The child was at the centre and learning was dynamic and interconnected. Critics, however, said that assessment was patchy and themes were often contrived and appealing more to the teacher than to the child.

The Scottish Storyline approach

The Primary Memorandum in Scotland (1965) and the Plowden Report (1967) encouraged teachers to have a curriculum with much more integration of different subjects like Maths, Literacy, History and Geography. At this time many teachers were unused to such freedom, creativity and autonomy. In Scotland, at Jordanhill College of Education, a group of tutors began an experiment that later gave birth to the Storyline approach. The pioneers of this approach were Steve Bell, Sallie Harkness and Fred Rendell. Their experiments on this thematic project approach to integrate the curriculum in a meaningful way gathered popularity and soon they were sharing the approach with colleagues in Germany, the Netherlands, Iceland and beyond.

This movement was initially given the title 'Storyline,' but this was adapted to 'the Scottish Storyline approach' as its popularity grew. It also spread to Denmark, Sweden, Norway, Finland, the Faroe Islands, Canada and the USA.

It is known in Denmark as *Den Skotske Metode*, and in Germany as *Die Methode Glasgow*.

This approach encouraged students and teachers to use a narrative to drive the learning. It saw Storyline as an authentic and enjoyable means of integrating learning across different curricular areas. The Scottish Storyline approach enabled teachers to develop ideas and approaches that bridged the gap between curricular areas. The approach was so transferrable that it helped learners in all cultures and languages and professions.

If you visit the website www.storyline-scotland.com you will see that the approach still thrives 50 years later.

This approach certainly thrived in the 1960s and early 1970s. The freedom and autonomy of the teacher, the progressive idea that learning could be shaped by the interests and curiosity of the learner, helped this holistic approach to develop learning in a much more interconnected way than had ever gone before.

The 1970s to 1980s

The next 20 years proved a challenging time for educators who were committed to the thematic or Storyline approach. The recession brought with it successive governments that tried to get more and more control over what was taught in schools. In England the mistrust of the 'progressive' movement caused policy to change and the curriculum became much more prescriptive.

In England the 1988 Education Reform Act called for a basic curriculum to be taught in all schools. This National Curriculum would set out attainment targets in knowledge, skills

18 *The theory, philosophy and approach*

and understanding that children would be expected at achieve. There would be 'programmes of study' taught at each stage. This National Curriculum would have three main subjects: Maths, English and Science; and six foundation subjects: History, Geography, Technology, Music, Art and PE.

Hence the demise of thematic approaches. Teachers had distinct subjects to deliver.

Dividing the curriculum up into discrete subjects like this made integrated 'topic' and 'project' work difficult, if not impossible. But perhaps the most damaging outcome of all was that it prevented teachers and schools from being 'curriculum innovators' and demoted them instead to be merely curriculum 'deliverers.'

The 1980s to 1990s

In Scotland: the 5-14 Curriculum

In the early 1990s the climate in education continued on its journey into accountability; a prescriptive curriculum and lots of emphasis on assessment were the order of the day in both England and Scotland. Teachers were to be made more accountable. Attainment was at the top of the agenda and so the curriculum guidelines became much more prescriptive. In Scotland the 5-14 Guidelines were introduced. National Assessments soon followed. Many critics suggested that the curriculum became so prescriptive that there was little room for teacher autonomy.

Whilst there was still scope in Scotland to explore thematic learning under the umbrella of Environmental Studies, many schools produced off-the-shelf topic packs in order to support staff to deliver a content-based curriculum.

During this period the teachers committed to maintaining the Storyline approach felt that they could still 'deliver' the curriculum simply by planning narratives that would enable pupils to learn the content set out in the guide. However, many were put off by this challenge. Teachers were under a good deal of pressure to cover a vast range of content and to get pupils through a wide range of tests.

In England: the National Curriculum

In England too there was a focus on accountability. A National Curriculum and SATs testing meant that similar pressures were put on the teachers who had previously had so much freedom and autonomy to develop thematic learning, based upon the pupils' interests and enthusiasm. Storyline had to take a back seat for a while with many teachers too overwhelmed to persevere.

And yet the approach survived, and in the UK, as well as in other countries around the world, this narrative approach was alive and well.

The 1990s

In Scotland: a Curriculum for Excellence and IDL

In the early 1990s there was a shift away from the prescriptive curriculum. In Scotland many of the principles of productive pedagogies (see the next chapter) were influential in creating a curriculum which was to develop attitudes and skills. This was the birth of a 'Curriculum for Excellence.' It was to be less content-driven and designed to give much more teacher and pupil autonomy. One of its key ideas was to have much more ownership of the learning resting with the learners themselves.

The principles of the Curriculum for Excellence have the 'Four Capacities' at their heart, and their purpose is often summed up as helping children and young people to become:

- successful learners;
- confident individuals;
- responsible citizens;
- effective contributors.

The curriculum has a focus on Outcomes and Experiences which emphasise a curriculum with much scope for child centredness, teacher autonomy and creative learning.

The Curriculum for Excellence then is designed to encourage different 'ways of learning.' Within the guidelines it includes four contexts for learning:

- curriculum areas and subjects;
- interdisciplinary learning;
- ethos and life of the school;
- opportunities for personal achievement.

So interdisciplinary learning is one of the key aspects of this new curriculum. Hence a resurgence in the interest in thematic approaches such as the Scottish Storyline approach.

At the time of writing the Curriculum for Excellence is still with us. Although there has been a tightening up of some of the content and a reintroduction of National Assessments, there is still plenty of scope for an integrated learning approach such as Storyline. Indeed, the requirement to deliver some sort of interdisciplinary learning gives teachers the mandate to think about this narrative approach towards integrating learning in different subject areas so that learning in Literacy, for example, might enhance learning in Music.

In England: a new National Curriculum

In England the picture is less clear. There is still a lot of prescription. There is still a lot of testing. However, the 2009 Independent Review of the Primary Curriculum had some comforting news. It stated that subjects, and the essential knowledge, skills and understanding they represented, were important but were not sufficient. Cross-curricular studies were important, too.

In the final report it states that:

> Our primary schools also show that high standards are best secured when essential knowledge and skills are learned both through direct, high-quality subject teaching and also through this content being applied and used in cross-curricular studies. Primary schools have long organised and taught much of the curriculum as a blend of discrete subjects and cross-curricular studies in this way.

20 The theory, philosophy and approach

This gives a clear mandate for taking an interdisciplinary approach. The report goes to some length to squash rumours that interdisciplinary or cross-curricular studies were not to be abolished:

> The proposal in my interim report to bring aspects of subject content together within areas of learning to facilitate cross-curricular studies was reported in some circles as 'abolishing subjects' such as history and geography. The reverse is true: subject disciplines remain vital in their own right, and cross-curricular studies strengthen the learning of the subjects which make up its content. From the standpoint of young learners, making links between subjects enriches and enlivens them, especially history and geography.

However, there is still a stance taken to preserve the traditional subjects in the National Curriculum:

> As indicated in the interim report, the essential knowledge and skills all children should be taught, particularly in the middle and later phases of primary education, can be organised through clearly visible subject disciplines, such as history, geography and physical education.

Though the report does go on to say:

> Subjects will be complemented by worthwhile and challenging cross-curricular studies that provide ample opportunities for children to use and apply their subject knowledge and skills to deepen understanding.

There does seem to be an understanding that learning needs to be within a meaningful context. Advocates of the Storyline approach would welcome these statements as they appear to provide a mandate for teaching through an authentic narrative approach:

> There are times when it is right to marshal content from different subjects into well-planned, cross-curricular studies. This is not only because it helps children to better understand ideas about such important matters as citizenship, sustainable development, financial capability and health and wellbeing, but also because it provides opportunities across the curriculum for them to use and apply what they have learned from the discrete teaching of subjects.
>
> Teachernet.gov.uk

Clearly then there is scope here for teachers to take an interconnected approach. The term 'cross-curricular' is used continually by these government documents, yet it is 'interdisciplinary learning' that is promoted in this book. I will explain what I see as the difference between these two terms later on in this book.

Taking a narrative, Storyline approach then is helpful in order to deliver the integration of subject-specific and interconnected learning required by the report.

Pendulum theory: Storyline and the curriculum

It might help to think of the curriculum, and curriculum reform, as a pendulum.

You can see from the summary above that in most of the UK the approach to the curriculum swung from a position of prescription and control in the 1940s and 1950s, with an emphasis on the teacher and the knowledge to be imparted, to the progressive movement in the 1960s, with the child at the centre, much more teacher autonomy and a more creative thematic approach towards teaching and learning.

In the 1980s and 1990s the pendulum swung back towards prescription, with much more government control over content, and teachers made accountable through national testing and a National Curriculum.

From 2000 to 2010 the swing shifted again, with acknowledgement of some of the damage done by over-testing children, and of the fact that learning needed to be more holistic and interconnected.

Since 2010 the shift has moved the other way again, with more testing introduced in Scotland – though introduced within a climate that maintains much teacher autonomy over what is taught and how it is to be taught.

No doubt the pendulum will continue to swing, but learning and the learner will continue to be the focus for future curriculum developments.

Storyline and the curriculum

Despite the many changes in the curriculum, there does seem to be an agreement that learning should be relevant and interesting. Most teachers and pupils would add that it should also be fun. In this book I hope to show how the curriculum – any curriculum – can be well explored through the narrative of a storyline.

Summary

In this chapter we have considered what is meant by *learning*. We have considered different ways of knowing and of organising learning in school. A brief history of the curriculum in England and Scotland revealed an ever-changing landscape shaped by the dominant theories and politics of each decade. One of the major issues is the debate about having single-subject learning in isolation and depth or instead having an interdisciplinary approach linking up the learning from different disciplines.

The debate will continue to be held and the curriculum will continue to change, pendulum fashion. I have suggested that the Storyline approach advocated in this book might be a futureproof way of enabling pupils to engage with the curriculum in an interesting and engaging way.

22   The theory, philosophy and approach

In the next chapter we will look at the way that pedagogy has changed and developed and how this can inform the curriculum and the way that it is interpreted in the classroom.

References

1965   Primary Education in Scotland (the Primary Memorandum)
1967   The Plowden Report
1988   Education Reform Act
2009   Independent Review of the Primary Curriculum

Websites

Storyline Scotland - www.storyline-scotland.com
Teachernet - teachernet.gov.uk/publications

3 Learning and pedagogy

In the last chapter we looked at the ever-changing curriculum and the way that this determines what is taught in the classroom. In many ways the role of the teacher can be defined by the curriculum that they are enlisted to implement. In this chapter we are considering the ways that the curriculum is implemented, enacted or delivered. Pedagogy is the method and practice of teaching. It is the 'how' that accompanies the 'what' – i.e. the curriculum is what we teach and pedagogy is how we teach it.

When we considered the history of the curriculum it was clear that in the post-war years content and knowledge were seen as the most important feature of the school timetable. For many reasons, including teacher shortages, the trends of the times, and educational theories, the most effective and efficient way to provide literacy, numeracy and knowledge in the classroom was through 'chalk and talk' – through direct teaching methods and often rote learning. The teacher was the master and the pupils were there as 'empty vessels,' ready to be filled with the knowledge and wisdom of the teachers. The teachers were to be all-knowing 'sages on the stage,' imparting knowledge to the eager learners. This situation could describe most schools and education systems from the 1950s to the 1960s.

Then, in the 1960s things began to change. There was a different view of the child as learner. Theorists suggested that the child should be at the centre. The teacher should be more of an enabler – 'a guide from the side.'

This was the age of progressive education. This was the age of change all over the world.

It was from the Primary Memorandum in Scotland in 1965, and the Plowden Report in England in 1967, that much of the philosophy of education that still prevails nowadays had its genesis. The child at the centre, the integration of learning, creative skills-based education, learning through play, and discovery methods all sprang from this 'progressive' movement.

In the classroom the teacher was given much more freedom. The knowledge and content were secondary to the skills, attitudes and creative approaches to be developed. For many this was a golden age.

As explored in the previous chapter this did not last. There followed over the 1970s, 1980s and 1990s a period of austerity – not just in society, but also in the role of the teacher. When the curriculum became far more prescriptive and goal orientated then so did the teaching. The pedagogy did not completely return to the didactic direct teaching of the 1950s but it certainly became less about the learning and more about the teaching.

Then, at the beginning of the 'noughties,' another revolution was emerging. It came from the Southern Hemisphere, with 'Productive Pedagogy.' This approach came out of a large commissioned research project funded by Education Queensland from 1988 to 2000. The study identified 20 classroom practices that would support both academic and social learning. These 'productive pedagogies' identified ways of teaching and learning that would get the best out of the learner. This was a nod back to the 1960s but with modern approaches and dispositions in mind.

This approach was a blend of Paulo Freire's Critical Pedagogy, Socratic Questioning of Thought, Bloom's Taxonomy and Gardner's Multiple Intelligence approach.

This Productive Pedagogy, like Scotland's Curriculum for Excellence (which was developed soon after) focused on four aspects or 'dimensions:'

- intellectual quality;
- relevance (or connectedness);
- socially supportive classroom environment;
- recognition of difference.

These terms are teased out on the TeacherSITY website: http://teachersity.org/newsletter/15-march/Pedagogy.html.

The essential message from Productive Pedagogy can be summarised in the table below:

Intellectual quality	Enhancing intellectual quality involves providing a challenging learning environment to learners that will engage them in big ideas and complex understandings
Relevance (or connectedness)	Relevance involves helping students to draw the connection between different aspects of school learning as well as connections with their past experiences and the real world
Socially supportive classroom environment	A socially supportive classroom environment involves providing an atmosphere that does not try to curb the enthusiasm of the learner. Instead it has high expectations from the learner, which motivates them to take risks in learning and encourages them to self-regulate their activities and learning
Recognition of difference	Recognition of difference encompasses inclusivity of non-dominant groups, and positively developing and recognising differences and group identities

> Productive Pedagogy reassembles our understanding of what good teaching is, and changes the emphasis from issues we've concentrated on in the past – the processes and techniques of the classroom, which are important, but not ends in themselves. It captures the essence of what is really important – a focus on student learning that's of high intellectual quality.
>
> New South Wales Department of Education and Training,
> quoted at teachersity.org

It is clear to see the shift away from teacher-led, content-driven pedagogy. It has a focus on the learner and their capabilities. It has an emphasis on 'making connections.' It strives to ensure that they receive high-quality learning. This book proposes that the Storyline approach can deliver these goals in an exciting and authentic way in the primary classroom.

It is clear to see how this approach also ties in with the Scottish Curriculum for Excellence with its four capacities:

- successful learners;
- confident individuals;
- responsible citizens;
- effective contributors.

The focus on the child and the interconnectedness of learning are stressed in both movements. Productive Pedagogy and the Curriculum for Excellence both provide clear links to taking an interdisciplinary approach to learning with the interests of the learner as a starting point.

At this point it is useful to take a closer look at the ongoing debate about pedagogy. There are arguments for and against taking this 'connected,' interdisciplinary approach. Some critics still argue that each curricular subject needs its own place in the curriculum. Others argue for an integration of the learning.

Integrated learning

The terms used to describe an integration of curricular learning are sometimes confusing. They sound similar but are all slightly different. You might come across 'cross-curricular', 'interdisciplinary', 'multi-disciplinary', 'integrated curriculum' and many more.

To be clear, let us try to establish a rough and ready definition for some of these so that we can properly understand the differences.

Term	Definitions	In plain English
Discipline	"A specific body of teachable knowledge with its own background of education, training, procedures, methods and content areas" (Berger 1970)	What is distinct about this kind of knowledge, this kind of learning, these approaches and attitudes?
	Each discipline is a distinct form of knowledge with separate and distinct characteristics (Hirst 1964)	Different ways of knowing
Cross-curricular	Involving curricula in more than one educational subject (Oxford English Dictionary)	Many elements of learning, taken from many different curriculum areas (see "The Potpourri Problem" below)
	An approach to a topic that includes contributions from several different disciplines and viewpoints (Collins English Dictionary)	
	"When the skills, knowledge and attitudes of a number of different disciplines are applied to a single experience, problem, question, theme or idea we are working in a cross-curricular way. The experience of learning is considered with *the curriculum as a focus*" (Barnes 2015)	It's all about learning in Maths, Science, Language or Art. The focus is on the knowledge/skills for that curricular area as opposed to on the topic itself

(continued)

(continued)

Term	Definitions	In plain English
Thematic learning	"[W]here at least part of the week is devoted to a particular theme or topic ... through the eyes of several curriculum subjects. The *stimulus* becomes the focus for learning" (Barnes 2015)	It's all about learning about the theme itself. The focus is on the theme itself as opposed to the knowledge/skills for that curricular area, i.e. it's all about the Vikings
Cross-disciplinary	"Viewing one discipline from the perspective of another; for example: the physics of music, the history of maths" (Miller 2012, citing Meeth 1978)	
Multi-disciplinary	"The juxtaposition of several disciplines focused on one problem with no direct attempt to integrate" (Miller 2012, citing Piaget 1972 and Meeth 1978), i.e. people from different disciplines working together, each drawing on their disciplinary knowledge	It's similar to *Cross-curricular* or *Interdisciplinary* but there is no attempt to integrate or make connections with the 'ways of knowing'
Transdisciplinary	"Creating a unity of intellectual frameworks beyond the disciplinary perspectives" (Jensenius 2012)	
Integrated learning	Used interchangeably with *Cross-curricular* and *Cross-disciplinary* and *Interdisciplinary* learning	Looking for ways to integrate the learning
Interdisciplinary	"A knowledge view and curriculum approach that consciously applies methodology and language from more than one discipline, to examine a central theme, topic, issue, problem, or experience" Jacobs (1989)	Where learning in one curricular area enhances and supports deep learning in another

Of course, this is a very complex subject and many academics have wrestled with some kind of definition. Jonathan Barnes (2015) suggests that:

> Interdisciplinary/cross-curricular teaching involves a conscious effort to apply knowledge, principles, and/or values to more than one academic discipline simultaneously.
>
> The disciplines may be related through a central theme, issue, problem, process, topic, or experience (Jacobs, 1989).
>
> The organizational structure of interdisciplinary/cross-curricular teaching is called a theme, thematic unit, or unit, which is a framework with goals/outcomes that specify what students are expected to learn as a result of the experiences and lessons that are a part of the unit.

According to Jeya Harish, Khrishnakumar and Dharma Raja (2012):

> There seem to be two levels of integration that schools go through: The first is integration of the language arts (listening, speaking, reading, writing, thinking) (Fogarty, 1991; Pappas, Kiefer, & Levstik, 1990); the second involves a much broader kind of integration, one in which a theme begins to encompass all curricular areas.

It is this much broader approach with many different curricular areas involved that draws a lot of criticism, however. Jacobs (1989) described this as a potpourri:

> *The Potpourri Problem.* Many units become a sampling of knowledge from each discipline. If the subject is Ancient Egypt, there will be a bit of history about Ancient Egypt, a bit of literature, a bit of the arts, and so forth.

She criticises this approach for its lack of focus. Indeed, when the integrated or thematic approaches first became popular in the primary school many teachers went overboard and contrived to put just about every curricular area into their topics. *Contrived* and *superficial* were the words used by Her Majesty's Inspectors to describe some of the worst of these.

Hence the tension between, on the one hand, the benefits of a cross-curricular approach – and on the other, the problem of a lack of depth and a superficial 'taste' of many different disciplines.

> Interdisciplinary/cross-curricular teaching is often seen as a way to address some of the recurring problems in education, such as fragmentation and isolated skill instruction.
>
> It is seen as a way to support goals such as transfer of learning, teaching students to think and reason, and providing a curriculum more relevant to students (Marzano, 1991; Perkins, 1991).
>
> Barnes (2015)

Hence also the popularity of the interdisciplinary approach. This is defined as having a particular focus on learning in more depth. Instead of six or seven elements in a traditional cross-curricular topic, the interdisciplinary approach may have its focus on only one or two different disciplines.

For example:

Traditional cross-curricular plan for 'the Vikings'

Activity	Learning
Research Viking ships	Reading for information
Make model longboat	Technology
Make and paint sails and shields	Art and design
Make poster about Viking gods	Religious study
Singing Viking songs	Music

It is clear that here the teacher is trying to cover a wide range of learning. They might indeed achieve all that they set out to do but how sure would they be about 'who learned what' in English, Music, RE, etc.? The chances are that it will all be very superficial and evidence will be rather weak.

Interdisciplinary plan for 'the Vikings'

Activity	Learning
Diary entry	Language
Describing what happened when the Viking raiders came to the island	Imagined personal writing in the style of a diary
Drama/discussion	Drama
A village meeting debating what should be done about the raiders	Teacher in role and hot-seating
	Expressing thoughts, feelings and ideas

In this example there is much more of a focus on the actual learning. The aim is to look in much more detail about the knowledge, skills and techniques. The assessment evidence should help to identify who is doing well and who will need support.

In the Scottish Curriculum the term 'interdisciplinary learning' is used confidently.

In England the term 'cross-curricular' is used throughout. We have looked at the difficulties in defining what the words actually mean and it is easy to see why the many terms explored are still used interchangeably.

Ultimately it might just come down to semantics. It is not essential to fully understand all of these terms. What is most important, however, is that you know what it is that you want the learners to learn and are able to show that they have actually learned it.

My approach is always to ask: have they learned what I wanted them to? If so, how do I know? What evidence of learning do I have?

Clearly you cannot provide satisfactory answers to these questions for every lesson when you are engaged in a cross-curricular approach involving many different curricular areas all at the same time. Hence the idea that a narrower focus, with learning in more depth, is more appropriate. If we devote our planning, teaching and assessment to two or three curricular elements, then we have much more chance of success. We will explore this idea of planning and assessment later on in this book.

What the critics say about interdisciplinary learning pedagogy

The benefits of such an approach include such comments as:

- It encourages learners to 'make connections.'
- Real life isn't divided up into disciplines.
- The purpose of learning is more evident.
- Understanding can be progressed on a variety of (subject) fronts.
- There isn't the space and time in the Primary Curriculum to do every subject in detail.
- Pupils are more motivated.
- There is more opportunity for collaboration and group work.

Thaiss (1986) stated that interdisciplinary learning puts children in the correct setting and environment to learn. Resnick (1989) proposed that cross-curricular learning increased the student's motivation and their level of engagement. He believed that within interdisciplinary learning the children see the value of what they are being taught, leading to them becoming more involved in the activity.

Interdisciplinary learning enables teachers and learners to make connections in their learning through exploring clear and relevant links across the curriculum.

It supports the use and application of what has been taught and learned in new and different ways and provides opportunities for deepening learning, for example through answering big questions, exploring an issue, solving problems or completing a final project.

It is claimed that interdisciplinary approaches provide learning that goes beyond subject boundaries, providing learners with the opportunity to experience deep, challenging and relevant learning:

> While subject matter content falls neatly into those discipline-based departments, students, unfortunately, do not compartmentalise themselves or their learning that readily.
> Fogarty (1991)

As you can see, many of these attributes of interdisciplinary learning are consistent with the productive pedagogies mentioned earlier. As this book hopes to prove, the Storyline approach is an excellent example of putting these benefits into practice. However, first let us consider what the critics who oppose an integrated curriculum have to say.

What the critics say: the challenges

One criticism is that terms like 'thematic,' 'interdisciplinary' and 'cross-curricular' are just a few of those that are used interchangeably with little clarity of what is distinct about each one.

Other criticisms include questions like:

- How can we join our thinking across subjects/disciplines if we haven't mastered any of the distinct features?
- Surely there will be a lack of depth to learning?
- Won't you just cover a lot of ground very superficially, and very little in depth?
- Won't you dilute the distinctiveness of the disciplines if you always lump them in a context along with other disciplines?
- What about learning for its own sake?
- How would you map interdisciplinary learning anyway?

Lindsay Paterson (quoted by Elizabeth Buie in *Tes*, 2009) claimed that,

> The fashionable orthodoxy ignored the need for direct teaching . . . and focused instead on the kind of applied inter-disciplinary project work which is supposed to displace the need for expertise.
>
> While inter-disciplinary work had its place, it made no sense unless the disciplines had been grasped first. Pupils could not grasp these fundamentals, if the 'didacticism of

the expert' was not available, and that depended on the teacher having the necessary disciplinary grasp.

He went on to say that:

- Learning how to learn is a crucial source of effective learning;
- But it works only if the learning is embedded in a discipline, with all its norms and values giving a framework of understanding;
- And, hence, although inter-disciplinarity is important, it makes no sense at all unless the disciplines have been grasped first.

Buie (2009)

Of course, in practice schools choose to steer a path that takes all of the arguments for and against into account. You will see the teaching of separate subjects and disciplines some of the time. There is no doubt that we do need to explore different ways of thinking and of seeing the world. There are different skills and concepts to be developed and consolidated. However, it is also acknowledged that learning is messy. It is interconnected. We need to develop learners who can think for themselves and who can be creative and resilient. The aim of productive pedagogies, the Curriculum for Excellence and the English National Curriculum is to have learners who can make connections and develop ideas and share them confidently with others. An interdisciplinary approach is one way to do this. Interdisciplinary learning, or thematic learning, or whatever you choose to call it, is now a fundamental pedagogy employed in schools all over the world.

The Storyline approach

This book is all about one way of developing this idea. It is called the Storyline approach.

It is clear that the Scottish Storyline approach can also deliver many of these dimensions:

- A narrative approach which gives pupils ownership over the story itself will provide learning that is relevant.
- A collaborative approach, which often has the pupils working in 'family' groups, supports the idea of a socially supportive classroom.
- A supportive ethos which helps to develop a 'can do' attitude where pupils take a risk and are creative in order to respond of the requirements of the storyline.
- A pedagogy which acknowledges that what is most important is the learner and the learner's learning.

Having considered the curriculum and pedagogy in terms of an interdisciplinary approach it is helpful now to consider some of the theoretical justification that can be found in support of the Storyline approach. Although most of the authors mentioned below wrote their theories after Storyline was introduced in schools, it is easy to see how its approach is entirely consistent with modern thinking.

Theoretical links and benefits of taking a Storyline approach

Vygotsky

If we look back many decades, at the time of the progressive movement, Vygotsky explored the idea that we learn best together. Learning is a social experience and often we can achieve much more if we have someone else to learn with. This notion was developed further by Johnson and Johnson.

Johnson and Johnson

Co-operative Learning has been around now for some time. Johnson and Johnson (quoted in Jacobs, Lee and Ng 1997) found that "students in cooperative learning settings compared to those in individualistic or competitive learning settings, achieve more, reason better, and gain higher self-esteem."

This approach is now widespread in our primary school classrooms – with the learning taking place in collaborative groups. These groups are often working together to solve a task. Often the work is of an interdisciplinary nature – the modern curriculum is now so overcrowded that teachers find it almost impossible to teach every subject separately.

Black and Wiliam, and Clarke

Approaches to teaching and learning changed drastically in response to *Inside the Black Box: Raising Standards Through. Classroom Assessment* by Paul Black and Dylan Wiliam.

The research led the way to pedagogies that made learning much more visible. Shirley Clarke popularised the research findings with a practical guide to establishing and sharing learning intentions and success criteria with the learner. This Formative Assessment movement established ways to create learning plans which involved the learner in a way that they had never before been included. The mysteries of assessment were replaced with a classroom ethos where the learners had much more power to influence not just what was learned, but also how it was learned and how it was assessed.

This notion of the learner at the centre echoes the Primary Memorandum. In Storyline the fact that the child has much ownership of the narrative and the authenticity of the story itself means that the learning is always clear and transparent.

Hattie and Dweck

More recently John Hattie has had a similarly important impact on classroom pedagogy. His work on Visible Learning has developed this notion that the learner should have ownership of the learning and much more responsibility for their own learning. In tandem with this, the work from Carol Dweck on Mindset has set the tone for developing an appropriate classroom climate and positive, resilient dispositions towards the learning process. Again, taking an interdisciplinary approach with a narrative-driven topic can deliver this kind of learning.

Tarrant and Holt

Along with my colleague Deb Holt, I have also done a lot of work on making learning visible and encouraging learners to support each other with 'peer learning interactions,' where learners are enabled to have meaningful conversations about how they learn. We have also developed many ideas for developing metacognition in the primary classroom (Tarrant and Holt 2015). This notion of articulating 'how to learn' can readily be integrated into a storyline where the pupils decide what they will learn and how they will find out. They also decide how to research and present what they learn. Having and developing the metacognitive capacity to explore themselves as learners is easily accommodated into a Storyline approach.

Summary

In this chapter we have considered some of the ideas and theories regarding learning itself. We have considered the way it has been developed in schools with a landscape of ever-changing pedagogies and curriculum guidelines.

We looked at pedagogy as the method and practice of teaching and how the ever-changing policy landscape has had an impact on what it is that the teacher does in the classroom. Productive pedagogies were discussed and links to a Storyline approach were established. The focus on the child and the interconnectedness of learning was stressed, and the tension between teacher autonomy and the constraints of a prescriptive curriculum.

We looked at integrated learning and the many different terms used to express this approach. We compared the 'potpourri' approach and the interdisciplinary approach, which has a more limited but sharper focus on the actual learning that is planned and assessed.

Finally, we explored what the critics have to say about this integrated approach, and links were then made to the theories that underpin the strengths of taking a narrative, Storyline approach.

One thing that seems consistent, however, is the notion of 'connected' learning. The rest of this book is an example of one approach to developing connected learners. The Storyline approach has survived turbulent times in education over many decades. It is popular and successful all over the world.

There will always be demands placed on the teacher to find ways to deliver the curriculum and to raise attainment. The thematic or Storyline approach strives to motivate learners and give them an interesting and often exciting way to learn.

The next chapter will show what it looks like in practice and how a teacher might employ it to develop the learning in the classroom.

The overwhelming response to the experience of learning through a Storyline approach is that of fun, enthusiasm, confidence, curiosity and enquiry. Such qualities prompted the subtitle of this book, *Learning with Passion*.

This approach has survived and thrived for decades, despite ever-changing curricula and changing demands put upon the education systems all around the world.

References

Barnes, J. (2015) *Cross-curricular Learning 3-14*. Thousand Oaks: Sage.
Buie, E. (2009) "Teaching in the Dock." *Tes*, 6 March.
Hirst, P.H. (1964) *Knowledge and the Curriculum*. London: Routledge and Kegan Paul.
Fogarty, R. (1991) "Ten Ways to Integrate Curriculum." *Educational Leadership*, 49(2): 61-65.
Gore, J., T. Griffiths and J.G. Ladwig (2001) "Productive Pedagogy as a Framework for Teacher Education: Towards Better Teaching." Callaghan: University of Newcastle.
Jacobs, G.M., C. Lee and M. Ng. (1997, June). "Co-operative learning in the thinking classroom." Paper presented at the International Conference on Thinking, Singapore.
Jacobs, H.H. (1989) "Interdisciplinary Curriculum: Design and Implementation." Alexandria: Association for Supervision and Curriculum Development.
Jensenius, A.R. (2012) "Disciplinaries: Intra, Cross, Multi, Inter, Trans." Retrieved from: www.arj.no/2012/03/12/disciplinarities-2/.
Jeya Harish, H.G, R. Khrishnakumar and B. William Dharma Raja (2012) "Cross-Curricular Connections: An Innovative Model for Curriculum Transaction." *Journal on School Educational Technology*, 7(3): 1-9.
Meeth, L.R (1978) "Interdisciplinary Studies: Integration of Knowledge and Experience." *Change*, 10: 6-9.
Miller, A. (2012) "Integration Strategies for PBL." Edutopia: www.edutopia.org/blog/integration-strategies-for-PBL-andrew-miller.
Piaget, J. (1972) *The Epistemology of Interdisciplinary Relationships*. Paris: Organisation for Economic Co-operation and Development.
Resnick, L. (1989) "Toward the Thinking Curriculum: An Overview," in Resnick, L., and L.E. Klopfer (eds), *Toward the Thinking Curriculum: Current Cognitive Research (1989 Yearbook)*. Alexandria: Association for Supervision and Curriculum Development.
Tarrant, P., and D. Holt (2016) *Metacognition in the Primary Classroom*. Abingdon: Routledge.
Thaiss, Christopher (1986). "Language across the Curriculum in the Elementary Grades." Urbana: ERIC Clearing House on Reading and Communication Skills, National Council of Teachers of English, Office of Educational Research and Improvement.

Other references

1965   Primary Education in Scotland (the Primary Memorandum)
1967   The Plowden Report

Websites

Storyline Scotland - http://www.storyline-scotland.com
Teachernet - teachernet.gov.uk/publications
TeacherSITY - http://teachersity.org/newsletter/15-march/Pedagogy.html

4 What does Storyline look like in the classroom?

In this chapter we will look at some of the questions people ask when they first hear about Storyline. Some of these are answered more fully in later chapters but if this is the first experience of Storyline you should find enough information here to persuade you that the approach is not as daunting as you might have feared.

What kind of storylines are there?

There are many kinds of storyline; in this book we focus on four main approaches but in truth there are too many to count. It all depends on what you want the class to learn and how well your imagination works in order to make the learning engaging and immersive. Taking the 'family' approach does enable them to identify with characters though, and this establishes a connection where the learners feel concern for the characters and what happens to them. This ownership and immersion – where the learners are willing to suspend some disbelief in order to enter into the storyline narrative – is what makes the learning potential so great.

Who is the approach designed for?

Although Storyline was originally designed to promote learning in the primary school it has also been used in different settings for different ages all over the world.

It has been used successfully in the police force, banking and in business.

On one course it was used for nurses and they created a 'super nurse' who did the perfect job. Participants were given scenarios and asked, "What would Super Nurse do in this situation?" The Storyline approach of creating a character to take on the narrative in an immersive situation has proved very popular all over the world. If you go to the Storyline Scotland website (www.storyline-scotland.com/what-is-storyline-2) you will see some of the many uses it has been put to since its inception back in the 1960s.

How to get started?

In this book we look at two ways you might do this – there are others but these should be enough to get you started.

One way is to start with a great idea and then try to justify this idea with reference to your curriculum. If you can show that taking the learners along this narrative can help to deliver the learning objectives and experiences, then off you go.

Alternatively, you might begin by looking at what it is that your curriculum is telling you needs to be covered (this is most useful in situations where your authority is quite prescriptive about what is to be learned – it might even be telling you when to teach this). Nevertheless, you might take this learning and then dream up a narrative that might enable the learners to become involved in an immersive narrative to deliver the learning. See Chapter 10 for more details on how to go about this planning process.

How long does it last?

This is a most difficult question! You can actually do a storyline in a day (see Appendix 1) or you can take several weeks. There is rarely a problem of 'keeping it going' – more often it is the storyline that is in danger of taking over! As the learners take ownership and their interests and immersion develop it can be difficult to tear them away!

However, if the teacher has a plan and keeps 'the line,' then a good rule of thumb would suggest 10 to 12 lessons either concentrated into a week or two or spread over a longer period. Sometimes the storyline provides a context for other learning – this is particularly useful if you work in a prescriptive environment where a strict curricular guide is to be adhered to. Through the storyline you can still do History and Maths and Reading at the usual timetabled slots – but what is different is that these lessons would all be thematically linked to the storyline narrative.

What does it look like?

A Storyline lesson generally involves a lot of fun and laughter. It requires the learners to communicate with one another (most of the time) and it involves problem solving, teamwork and negotiating skills. In fact, many of the soft skills required nowadays by industry are involved in a successful storyline.

Storyline lessons can look just like any other – see above regarding History, Maths, etc., or alternatively it can look more like a collaborative group challenge with pupils moving around the classroom engaged in their learning. Lessons will not all look the same, but it is the teacher who will decide how they look and what pedagogy is used to make them engaging and successful.

Organisation, pedagogy and practice

As mentioned above, the teacher can select what they feel is the best method and pedagogy to deliver the learning for each lesson. Every storyline is different and it is likely that there will, over a series of lessons, be some group work, individual work, reading, writing, speaking and listening. Often there is a lot of art work and creative elements to the story. Often there is drama and always some sort of celebration to finish things off. This might take the form of an exhibition, a party or drama performance or sharing of work.

How do the learners react?

One of the amazing things about taking a narrative approach is the fact that the learners really do get carried away with enthusiasm. Storyline classrooms are characterised by the sound of laughter, a lively hubbub of discussion and a real sense of enquiry. The emphasis on listening and talking means that these classrooms are rarely silent, but it is a climate of positive noise and total immersion. As Caitlin in Primary Seven puts it, "This is a really great way to get us learning because we are having so much fun that we don't even notice that we are working!"

Because the Storyline approach is so inclusive, with many activities that come with open-ended tasks which remove the fear of failure, it is easier for all pupils to get involved and to feel ownership of the learning.

Feedback from teachers

- One of the things that struck me was the fact that they could talk and learn things that I could never have planned for. They really got into their characters and were able to interpret events from a particular point of view.
- My class are really buzzing – so excited about their alien friend!
- I'm really nervous, I have chainsaw sound effects and a smoke machine ready, and after break I plan to burn their rainforest!!

Evidence of learning

Later in this book there is a chapter that explores what evidence will look like and how a teacher might go about providing evidence of progress. Mapping out the actual learning is something that was always a challenge when using the traditional topic approach – particularly when it was an all-embracing project that aspired to fit in as many curricular areas as possible. Instead of spreading the learning so thinly over many curricular areas, this book advocates taking a more focused approach where there are two or three areas targeted. Within this there are clear learning outcomes and success criteria so that mapping the learning should be much more meaningful and manageable. See the chapters on planning and assessment for more details on this subject.

Recording and assessment

In Chapter 11 we will take a detailed look at some of the different ways to evidence the learning, from observations of listening and talking to presentations and drama productions. There are the things that the learner might say, make, write and do. In this chapter we also look at some possible approaches towards creating a systematic means of recording these assessments.

Clearly it is essential that learning takes place and that there is some record of progression through this learning. A storyline can appear to be led and controlled by the enthusiasm of the learners – they do indeed hold the story. However, it is the teacher who must keep a tight rein on the line – the learning. Most of what happens in a storyline happens because the teacher has created a meaningful context for the learning. Often this is augmented by the incidental learning that, although not planned, occurs and is significant and relevant enough to be added to the plans retrospectively. This control over the learning, both planned and incidental, is what informs the assessment. This approach enables Storyline to be used to implement even the most prescriptive of curriculum objectives.

Involving the learners

As mentioned earlier, this approach enables the learners to be fully involved. While the teacher holds the 'line' or the curricular outcomes, it is the learner who has the story. They have ownership of the direction that the narrative follows, and feel like they can make meaningful decisions about what happens and what they learn. They are active participants in this learning and they work with a true sense of audience and purpose.

What if?

> What if my school is very prescriptive and insists that I deliver curriculum and content that has been tried and tested, yet I want to try a Storyline approach?

Why not take a look at the content and skills that need to be covered and create a storyline that will do the same job as the traditional approach (but hopefully in a more immersive and engaging way)? It is likely that you will be judged by pupil engagement and enthusiasm and by the results of their efforts. If you can inspire them to learn with passion and can collect the assessment evidence of their progress you should be 'allowed' to use what you see as the most productive pedagogy at your disposal.

> What if the class get so wound up that they actually believe that the storyline is all true?

Clearly there is a possibility that you might go too far. In reality, though, it is unlikely that they will actually believe and go on believing. Often they guess that this is a fantasy but they engage nevertheless. If it looks like some will be disappointed when they find out then you might need to start letting them down gently rather than all at once at the end of the topic.

> How can I keep tabs on all of the learning if it is all done through group work and the emphasis is on talking?

Well, it isn't all done through groups and through talk. Yes, this can be an aspect of a storyline, but as you will see in the plans and examples later in this book there are also individual tasks and evidence. We will also look at ways of gathering assessment evidence and keeping a comprehensive record of who is learning what.

Summary

In this chapter we have considered what a Storyline project might look like in the classroom. We have explored some of the key concerns for teachers when they come across this approach.

Having established some basic idea of what a storyline looks like, how we might go about it, how long it might take and how we might assess and evaluate it, we can now move on to investigate some of these issues in more detail in the rest of this book.

Part II
Four approaches to planning a storyline

5 The Street
A WWII storyline, plan and process

Introduction

In this chapter you will find a detailed, but by no means definitive, plan for a storyline on the topic of World War II (WWII). It is not intended to be a plan to be strictly adhered to by the teacher, but merely an example in detail to show how a narrative can be used to drive the learning. The most important thing to remember, as with any storyline, is that the teacher has always a clear hold of the line: that is, the learning that is intended for the pupils. This should include strategies for the assessment of that learning: whether that be in terms of observation notes on the process and the attitudes of the learners, or through records of the assessment of the product of the learning; for example, work on the classroom display, in their jotters, and letters or artwork produced in response to the storyline narrative.

Once this concept of the teacher holding this line is clearly understood then the teacher can allow the class to take the story. So, in the plan detailed below it might be that the children's interests take a different path. They might show an interest in something else. They might have ideas for their characters that take the story in a different direction. If so, it is important to remember that the lesson ideas, and the lesson order set out below, are only important in so far as they deliver the learning. So it does not matter if, for example, the plan to bomb one of the houses does not seem appropriate at the time, as long as you are still able to steer them to want to research something about the Blitz and the subsequent evacuation and its impact on their characters. The story order and events can be changed and adapted – but the 'learning' needs to be clearly realised. It is about the *learning*, not the activities!

For the participants it should feel like it is all about them and their story experience. For the teacher it should be all about how to accommodate their enthusiasm and interest and yet keep a clear focus on the learning.

WWII storyline plan and process

Lesson 1: what do we want to find out?

1   Introduce the topic to the class and begin with a KWL grid (see below).

Four approaches to planning a storyline

What do we already know about WWII?	What do we want to find out?	How can we find out?	How can we record this information?

A good way to do this is to have a 'brainstorming' sheet of paper or get the class into groups, each listing things that they know, and gathering key questions from them.

2   From this information you can then establish a few key questions for the class to investigate, such as:
   - Why was there a war?
   - Which countries were involved?
   - What did Hitler want?
   - Did we need the Americans in order to win?
   - What happened at the end of the war?

3   Once the key questions have been established you can focus on exploring ways to find answers and discussing ways information might be recorded and shared.

Teacher planning

This introduction to the topic can help to generate interest and an overall sense of direction. Afterwards the teacher should consult the curriculum documents to find out which learning experiences might be targeted through the vehicle of the topic. For example, in the Scottish Curriculum for Excellence you might choose:

> SOC 2a-01a: "I can use Primary and Secondary sources selectively to research events in the past."
>
> ENG 2-30a: "As I write for different purposes and readers I can describe and share my experiences, expressing what they made me think and how they made me feel."

This particular topic provides scope for much learning under the heading of Social Studies and Literacy. It is also possible to touch upon aspects of RME and Art & Design. However, it is important to have a focus on only two or three curricular areas in depth rather than many more covered in a more superficial manner.

Lesson 2: the families

Lesson 2 can be the introduction of the storyline. A good way to introduce the story is to read an extract from an appropriate children's novel such as *The Machine Gunners*, *Goodnight Mister Tom* or *When Hitler Stole Pink Rabbit*. This provides an opportunity to set the scene and hook the reader in.

1. Tell the class that they are to imagine that they are living around 1940 at the time of WWII. In their groups they are to be a family living in Glasgow. (It is useful to choose Glasgow as there were air raids on the shipyards there and this gives scope for the story to be both dramatic and authentic. Clearly there are many other cities in Britain where similar events took place, so somewhere closest to the homes of the pupils will enable them to be properly immersed in the narrative.)
2. Each person in the group has to be a family member. They can be anyone they want but should aim to have a mixture of male, female, adult and child.
3. Pupils are given templates to draw around and decorate as members of the family. (At this point they might ask what kind of clothes they wore. The teacher can provide books and photographs to guide them or they could be given the task of researching this. However, as it would take some time for the children to locate the information this can take away from the pace and impact of the lesson, so it is probably best to provide the information on this occasion.)
4. Each family can be assembled into group portraits. The children will be asked to introduce their characters and to tell the class something about them.
5. Each family will be displayed on the wall. The teacher will also create a family to go alongside them.

44 *Four approaches to planning a storyline*

Lesson 3: the characters

1. For the next lesson there are a number of possibilities. It is important to develop a 'relationship' between each child and their created character. This can be done by having a lesson where they are guided to create biographies or fact files for their character. They can record the name, age, occupation, hobbies and personal characteristics for their character. A passport can be created.
2. In order to keep the story authentic, you might look up common names for children born in the late 1930s. You could also give the pupils a list of common surnames for their area and also common occupations. This background information could be researched by the groups themselves or provided by the teacher. (In order to get things going swiftly I personally prefer to provide this information and then include research activities later on in the project.)
3. This information should help them to begin to relate to their families and to imagine what it might have been like for families in the 1940s. The groups could then go on to develop an imaginary personal diary entry about a day in the life of their character.
4. Some group and class discussion can be developed with scenarios explored where each member of the family reacts to a simple event like the ones detailed below:

    How do the characters react and what do they do when . . .

    a   they run out of milk (where would they go to get some? What would the shops be like?);
    b   they need the toilet (where would they go? What would it be like?);
    c   going out to play (where will they go? What will they do?);

d   having a bath (where would they go? What would it be like?);
e   someone has a bad fall and has to go to hospital (what would the hospital, the treatment and the medicine be like?).

At the end of this lesson the pupils will have explored and developed their characters and produced a piece of writing for the display which provides some information about their character.

Lesson 4: the homes

Having established the characters and some of their 'history' and personalities it is time to create their homes.

1   Tell the class that their families live in a street on the banks of the River Clyde in Glasgow (or an alternative site where there was some threat from the Blitz.) You might show them some photographs from the time, and a map. On the classroom display you should have a frieze ready with the river, possibly some tall cranes for the shipyards in the distance, and of course space for the street to go.
2   In order to have everything in proportion it is helpful to provide some guides at to the size of each house. An easy way to do this is to provide a template – which could be as simple as a rectangle for the house and another as the basis for the roof. Each group can personalise and decorate their home based on photographs and pictures provided by the teacher.

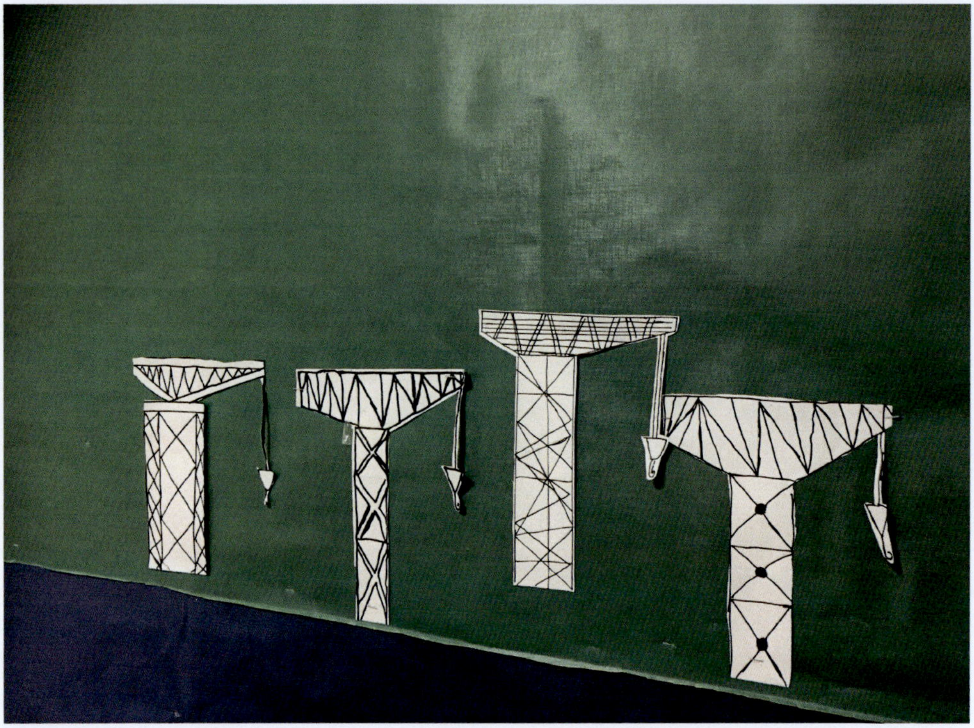

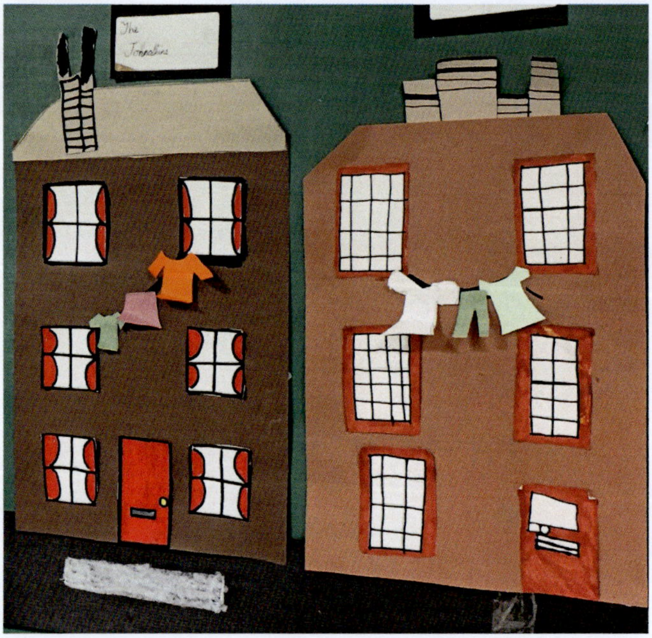
The

3   The teacher should also create a home for their own family and place it near to the middle of the street. The pupils will then add their own homes in a line with the rest.
4   At this point it is good to discuss some of the things that might be needed in the street. This can range from street furniture like lamp posts and a post box to amenities like a corner shop or school. These can be added to the frieze if space allows.

Lesson 5: ordinary daily life

1   The next phase of the storyline is designed to enable pupils to learn about what society was like at the time of the storyline. Each family is encouraged to research, record and present information about what ordinary life would have been like for their family in that street at that time.
2   The pupils will be encouraged to find out what their homes were like, what amenities did they have and where they would go for provisions. Employment and schooling would be explored too.
3   This information could be presented as a piece of writing, a drama, a PowerPoint display or as a short media clip created by the family.

Lesson 6: an event – a letter from the Ministry

1   The children arrive in the classroom to a letter on their tables. The letters are only addressed to the males in the families that are 18 or over. They are being sent to war! In their family groups there will be a discussion about how this would make them feel.
2   Included in this group of conscripted soldiers will be at least two from the family created by the teacher. (This will provide a device for encouraging the class to find out about the events of the war as these two soldiers will post letters telling them about some of the battles, asking them some things to find out, etc.)
3   The conscripted will go off to war. Their destinations will be shown on a display map of Europe with the characters moved to the map. (Again, the events of WWII can be moved along as letters from the front arrive.)

Lesson 7: the bombers and the shelter

1   The pupils come into the classroom to see that a number of bombers have been added to the frieze.
2   On their tables are leaflets on how to build an Anderson shelter in your garden, and (for this lesson) how to build a model of an Anderson shelter.
3   As they build their shelters the children will discuss what it would have been like to be in the shelter during an air raid.
4   It might be possible to also discuss what you had to do if there wasn't time to go to the shelter: go under the kitchen table. You could play the siren sound on the Smartboard and tell the class to quickly get under the tables!

Lesson 8: the Blitz

1. In this lesson the class can be engaged in learning about some of the events from WWII – possibly in response to letters from characters at the front.
2. They will be reminded that if the siren goes off they must get beneath the tables.
3. The frieze will be covered up during this lesson.
4. At some point the siren will go and as the class hide below the desks sound effects of falling bombs will be played. The teacher will remove the material that has been obscuring the frieze and when the all clear is sounded they will see that bombs have fallen on their street.
5. There will be very little left of the teacher's house and the houses nearby will be badly damaged.
6. The class will be told that, although their families were safely in the shelter, the teacher's family were hiding in the house and did not survive.
7. At this point the pupils will be asked to direct the learning: what do they want to do? Should they repair the house? Hold a funeral? Have a street meeting about keeping everyone safe? Should they decide to make sure everyone is reminded about using the shelter whenever the siren goes?
8. There is potential for much learning here in Literacy, Social Studies, Health and Wellbeing and even RME.
9. The class can be told about how the raids on the Clyde destroyed many houses and some of the shipyards. They can see old photos and some video footage of the raids and the aftermath.

Lesson 9: evacuation

1. When the pupils come into the classroom each family will find a letter (addressed to the head of the household – the man!). The letter will tell them that it is no longer safe for the children to stay in the street and that they are to be evacuated to the country; for example, many of the children from Glasgow were sent to a place in the Borders called Peebles. The families will discuss what this means and how it makes them feel. Drama work could be done to draw out what happens when a child says they won't go or a mum is angry or upset about the letter.
2. Each group will be given a suitcase-shaped piece of paper and the family will help the children to pack. You might even get them to make a gas mask and a label for the journey.
3. More drama can be created by using a big space (like the hall) and giving the children gas masks and cases. The adults in each family can form a line as if on the platform of the station to say goodbye. 'Hot seating' or 'conscience alley' can be used to have each character to articulate how they would be feeling.
4. Once the imaginary train has left, this scene can be mirrored with each family pretending to be the folks of Peebles waiting for the train of evacuees to arrive.
5. When the train gets in, the children line up. The adults will select a child (not from their own families). Ideally some children would be split up from siblings to mirror what would have happened in real life.

6   Again, the scope for drama and for imaginary writing here is immense. There could be follow-up activities involving different genres of writing – letters, diary entries, journals, newspaper articles – all based on the evacuees being away from home as the war goes on.
7   The film/novel *Goodnight Mister Tom* would be very useful here to convey many of the feelings experienced by the families in this situation.

Lesson 10: street party

1   In the final lesson the class need to know that the end of the war is near. This might be introduced through letters from the front, or from some of the characters arriving home to a hero's welcome.
2   Watching footage of the end of the war could also be a means of exploring this.
3   The class would then be asked how they would like to celebrate the end of the topic. They might want to plan and hold a street party of their own, or they may wish to display all the work they have been doing and invite other classes (and parents) to their own exhibition.

Project review

After the project has ended and been celebrated it is important to have a review of what the class have learned from the experience. It is important to explore the skills, knowledge, attitudes and dispositions that have been developed.

This can be done through discussion, mind-mapping or poster-making or by completing a carousel activity to gather impressions from the learners about what they learned and how they learned it.

Other ideas

In tandem with the ideas above the teacher might use their own invented 'family' to advance the learning in terms of the key questions provided by the class.

For example, the teacher can tell them about how 'Alfie' and 'Albert' were asking their dad about Hitler. Alfie wanted to know why Hitler had started the war.

The teacher could then ask the class to do some research into the start of the war and to try to answer the question. Once they have some information they would be asked to select a way of sharing this with 'Dad' so he could satisfy the curiosity of his children.

This could be done through a piece of writing, a poster, a PowerPoint presentation or any other means of communication that the class had some experience of. This could be built into the project as a way of hitting curricula targets in writing and literacy.

Another possibility would be to have someone in one of these families working for the Ministry. They could come home saying, "How can we encourage people to use the air raid shelters? How can we get people to dig up their gardens and plant veg to help with the food shortages?" The class could then work on propaganda posters and leaflets.

In terms of the pupils learning some of the historical facts of the war, the narrative might be driven by the use of newspapers. At the start of each episode the pupils could be greeted by a newspaper cover telling them the latest events of the war. This device can drive the narrative and invite questions and a search focus for the class.

Summary

In this chapter we have had a detailed look at one approach towards a storyline narrative. This idea of using a family and a place is a very common device for getting the learners immersed in the story and to give them a sense of connection and ownership of their learning. Using this approach there are many storylines that are possible. Below is a list of just a few of them. Each time the class will go through a similar process to that above:

- the hook to get them interested;
- creating a person and family from that time and place;
- creating homes;
- establishing what ordinary daily life was like;
- an event or problem;
- a solution and celebration;
- a review of the learning.

Storyline and the past

This can be done on topics like 'WWII' or 'WWI,' 'the Vikings,' 'the Normans,' 'Castles,' 'the Highland Clearances,' 'the Romans,' 'the Victorians' or 'the Tudors.' In fact, any topic set in the past. (See more examples in the Appendices.)

Storyline and the present

Alternatively, you might look to a place and situation in the present – from famine to refugees to new neighbours, you can create a context for the pupils to imagine being in a family in their situation. (See more examples in the Appendices.)

Storyline and the future

Similarly, the narrative can be imaginative and speculative: they can imagine they are a family living in the future or a group of volunteers sent to colonise another planet. The possibilities are only restricted by your imagination – the format will work for any of these ideas. As long as you have a clear focus on the learning and the curriculum to be explored then anything is possible using this approach. (See more examples in the Appendices.)

In the next chapter we will look at another approach towards creating a narrative: the Letter.

6 The Letter
The Owl Who Was Afraid of the Dark and a Health and Wellbeing storyline

Introduction

In this chapter we will look at another strategy for developing a narrative approach towards learning. Instead of using a family and a street we can use the convention of a letter to drive the story along. With links to other curricular areas a letter to the learners can prompt interest and enquiry in the class. A letter can get them interested and immersed and they can be invited to help the author of the letter to find information, solve a problem or give advice. In this way the learners can imagine themselves in a different (often difficult) situation and work out what they might do in the circumstances. Whether it is 'lost in the woods' or being bullied at school or abandoned in a strange place, they can identify with the character and try to come up with possible solutions. The letter(s) can come from someone real or from a character in a book or from the TV.

In this chapter we will look in detail at a storyline aimed at Early Years pupils and based upon a well-known novel, *The Owl Who Was Afraid of the Dark*, and another storyline aimed at older children, based on a letter from another school asking the class for help and information.

The owl storyline project

The Owl Who Was Afraid of the Dark is a novel used often in the early years. It features a rather timid owl who worries a lot.

The day before the storyline begins the class will have had a look at some of the book. They will have engaged in discussion about the topic in general, in preparation for the surprise to come the following day.

Lesson 1

The next day the teacher prepares with a box containing a few feathers and the message for the class. The box is profiled by having a trail of feathers leading up to it for the class to 'discover' when they enter the classroom.

Teacher: Now, boys and girls, somebody has noticed something unusual in our classroom today. These feathers were not here before break time. And they lead to this strange box! Remember the story we had yesterday about the owl? Well, I wonder if these are owl feathers? Why do you think they are here? Any ideas?

At this point there can be a discussion to reactivate their prior knowledge and to assess what they recall from the story the day before.

Teacher: Let's see what is in the box. Oh, look: a rolled-up piece of paper, and it's a letter! A letter from someone. Let's read it.

The letter asks the class if they will help the owl to overcome a fear of the dark. In this example the teacher was also wanting to do some work on firework safety, so there was also a request for the class to help the owl to stay safe.

> Dear Boys and Girls,
>
> Hello,
>   My name is Plop and I'm a baby Barn Owl. I have a story written all about me and my fear of the dark and I was hoping you could read it?
>   Also, I'm really hoping you can help? I've been hearing so many loud bangs at night recently and I think it might be something called 'fireworks'. I have seen them once before but don't know much about them, can you help?
>
> Yours sincerely,
Plop

Four approaches to planning a storyline

> The Tall Tree
> The Faraway Forrest
> Storyland
> 04.11.2016
>
> Dear Boys and Girls,
>
> Hello, my name is Plop and I'm a baby Barn Owl. I have a story written all about me and my fear of the dark and I was hoping you could read it?
>
> Also, I'm really hoping you can help? I've been hearing so many loud bangs at night recently and I think it may be something called 'fireworks'. I have seen them once before but don't know much about them, can you help?
>
> Yours sincerely,
>
> Plop

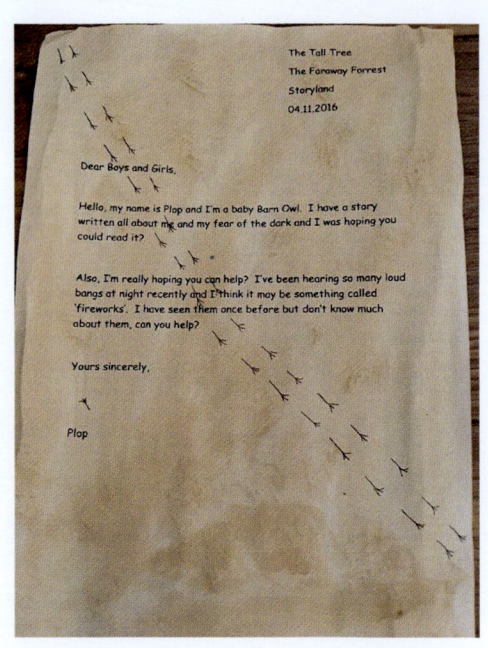

The class can then be invited to see if they can help. They can be guided to come up with the idea to write back to Plop. In the example below they decided to write back to Plop with an explanation of what fireworks were and how they sometimes made the children feel.

At this point you might be thinking, what if they don't believe me? What if they do believe me completely? In reality younger children do believe – they want to believe to begin with and evidence like the feathers helps them to suspend their disbelief. Occasionally you might get one or two who ask you, "Is it really from the owl?" At this point you might simply be evasive and turn the question back on them: "Well, there are feathers, and it does sound like an owl. What do you think?"

In our example the letter from Plop prompted a lot of discussion. The pupils then created a mind map of emotions and ideas associated with feeling scared. This was produced as a scaffold to the letters they later wrote to Plop with reassurance and advice.

The class then worked on some pictures in order to explain what fireworks were.

Clearly the learning here isn't just in terms of literacy, talking, listening and writing, but also in art techniques.

In this first phase of the storyline it is important to create the illusion of the character seeking help. In order to make it an immersive experience you do need to imply that it is real, whilst at the same time avoiding any definitive answer; for example:

Child: Is it really a letter from the owl?
Teacher: I'm not sure. What do you think?
Child: I don't believe it was the owl – owls can't write!
Teacher: Well, it is important that you believe what you want but let's not spoil the fun for everyone else.

.10.16.

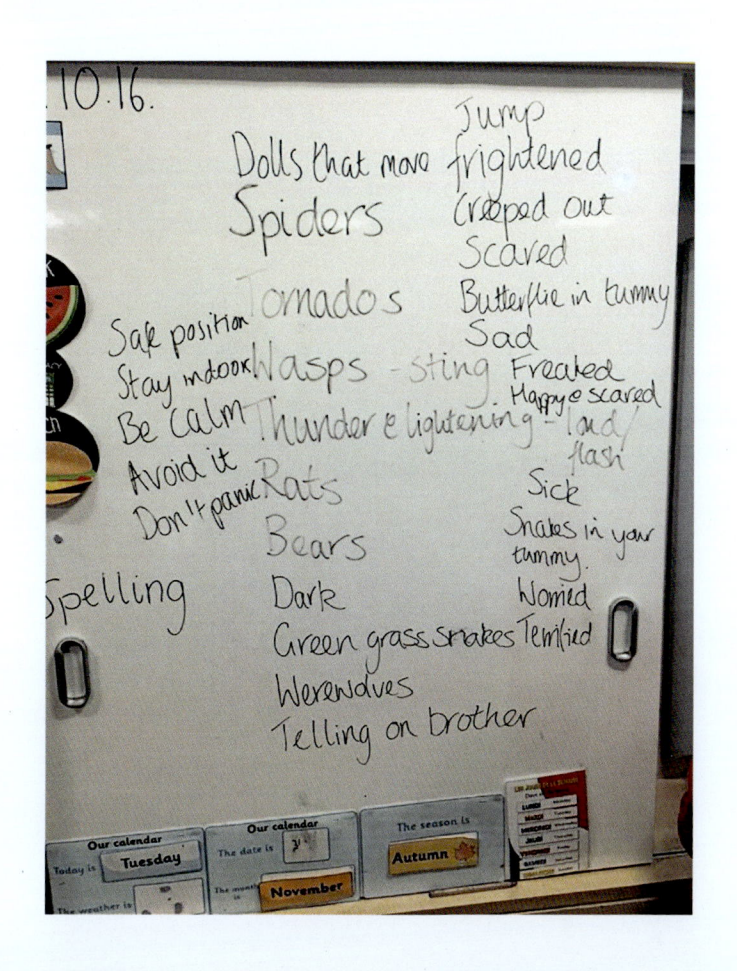

Dolls that move — Jump / frightened
Spiders — Creeped out / Scared
Tornados — Butterflies in tummy / Sad
Safe position
Stay indoors — Wasps - sting — Freaked
Be Calm — Thunder & lightening — Happy & scared / loud / flash
Avoid it
Don't panic — Rats — Sick
Bears — Snakes in your tummy
Spelling
Dark — Worried
Green grass snakes — Terrified
Werewolves
Telling on brother

Our calendar — Today is Tuesday
Our calendar — The date is / The month is November
The season is Autumn

Lesson 2

It is important to establish a dialogue between the class and the owl. Whenever the class are tasked to do something or to find something out it is important to have Plop provide some kind of feedback.

The next day there was another trail of feathers and a new note from Plop.

Dear Boys and Girls,

Thank you for your firework pictures, they were beautiful! I was really happy to hear that my story had helped you all think about your feelings and talk about what you were scared of. I really enjoyed hearing about what you did to make yourselves feel better.

As you did such a good job I was wondering if you could help me? I really want to find out more about other feelings and as I have no one here that can help, I was wondering if you all could?

Yours sincerely,
Plop

The Tall Tree
The Faraway Forrest
Storyland
08.11.2016

Dear Boys and Girls,

Thank you for your firework pictures, they were beautiful! I was really happy to hear that my story had helped you all think about your feelings and talk about what you are scared of. I really enjoyed hearing about what you all did to make yourselves feel better.

As you all did such a good job I was wondering if you could help me? I really want to find out more about other feelings and as I have no one here that can help, I was wondering if you all could?

Yours sincerely,

Plop

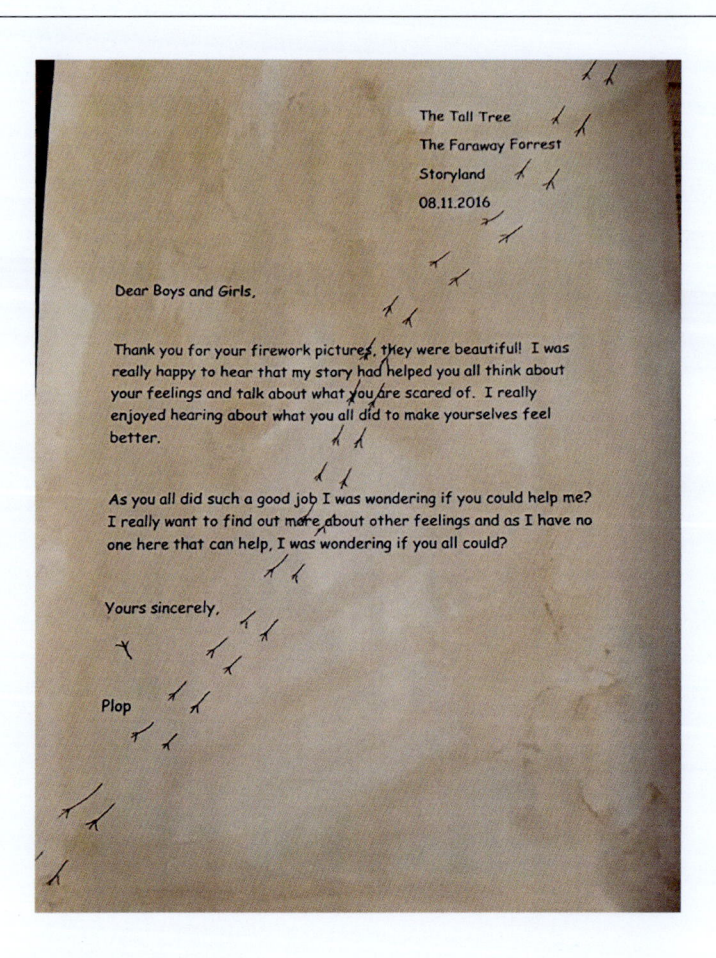

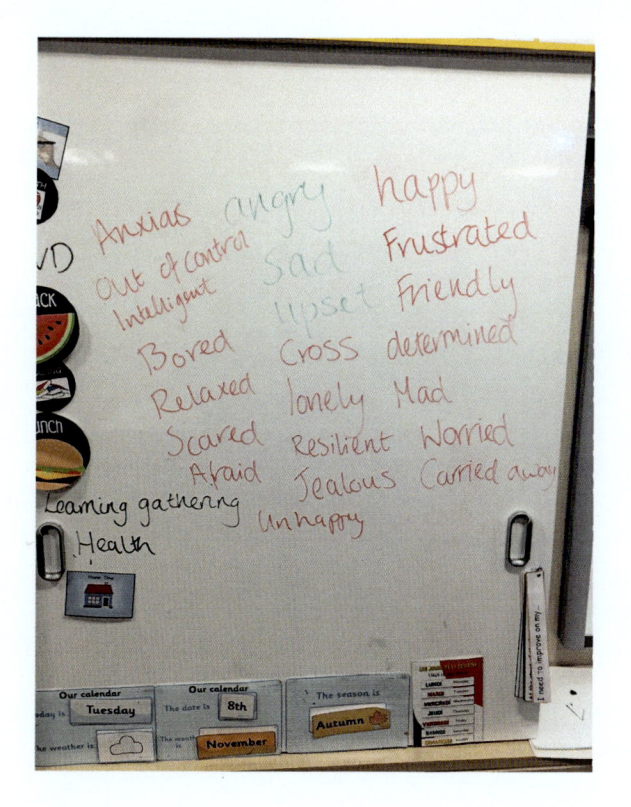

Anxious angry happy
Out of control Sad Frustrated
Intelligent Upset Friendly
Bored Cross determined
Relaxed lonely Mad
Scared resilient Worried
Afraid Jealous Carried away
Learning gathering Unhappy
Health

Again, there was scope for much learning in terms of listening, talking, writing and artwork.

The class had discussion work, made face plates (paper party plates with facial expressions to reflect their emotions) and wrote letters back to Plop.

The next step was to try to encourage and develop the research skills of the class. Along with the now-customary trail of feathers there was a blanket left by the teacher's chair. Under the blanket was a basket of resource books that would help the class with the next task.

Dear Boys and Girls,

I wanted to thank you so much for your response to my last letter. You really helped me learn about other feelings and I really enjoyed seeing your pictures and face plates and reading your letters.

I have another problem that I hope you can assist me with? As some of you know, I am a nocturnal animal and my friends and I don't think that people know enough about us. As we only come out at night there's lots of people who have never seen us and I was hoping that you could help to share who we are with some interesting facts about us? I've left you lots of information about us and I am hoping that you can come up with a way to share it.

Yours sincerely,
Plop

The class had to find information in the reference books, record their findings and decide on the best way to share what they had learned. Some wrote letters, others chose to make posters and others included the information in a fact file or greetings card. All were developing skills in researching, selecting, recording and presenting non-fiction information.

The interaction and dialogue with Plop was continued with this response:

Dear Boys and Girls,

I wanted to say a really big thank you for your excellent booklets and posters you made about my nocturnal friends! They were great and had so much information on them, they will definitely help in sharing who we are and what we do.

Myself and my bat and hedgehog friends are so grateful for what you have done for us and hope that you can continue to share your knowledge.

I therefore only have one last request for you all: could you share the booklet and posters you have made with some others?

Yours sincerely,
Plop

The Tall Tree
The Faraway Forest
Storyland
14.11.16

Dear Boys and Girls,

I wanted to thank you so much for your response to my last letter. You really helped me learn about other feelings and I really enjoyed seeing your pictures and face plates and reading your letters.

I have another problem that I hope you can help me with? As some of you know, I am a nocturnal animal and my friends and I don't think that people know enough about us. As we only come out at night there's lots of people that have never seen us and I was hoping that you could help to share who we are and some interesting facts about us? I've left you lots of information about us and I am hoping that you can come up with a way to share it.

Yours sincerely,

Plop

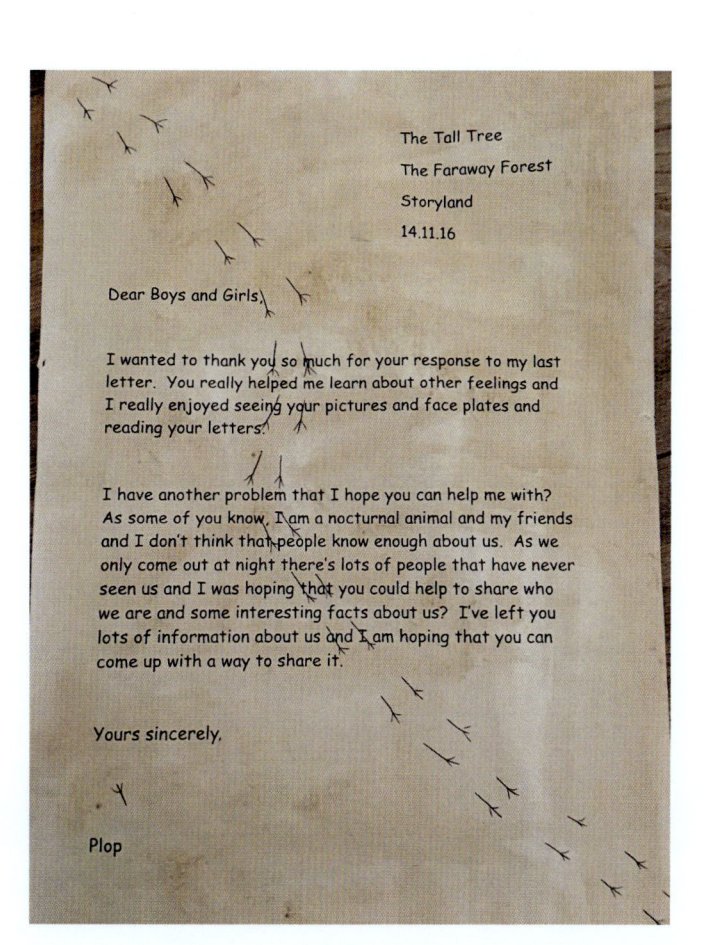

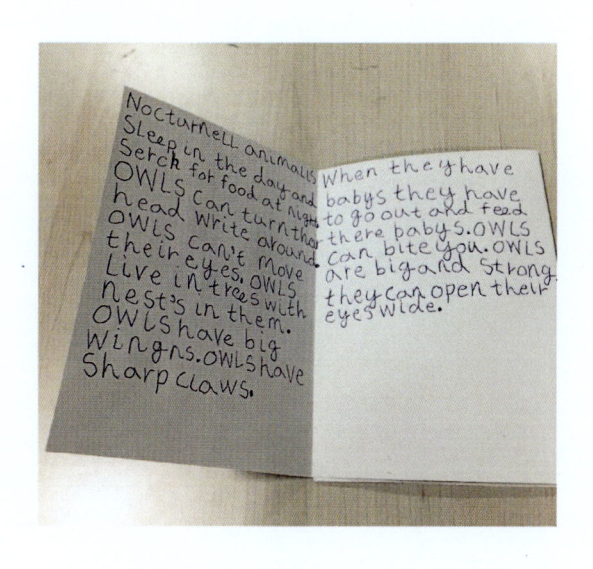

Nocturnell animalls sleep in the day and serch for food at night. OWLs can turn thor head write around. OWLs can't move their eyes. OWLs live in trees with nest's in them. OWLs have big wingns. OWLs have sharp claws.

When they have babys they have to go out and feed there babys. OWLs can bite you. OWLs are big and strong, they can open their eyes wide.

OWLS

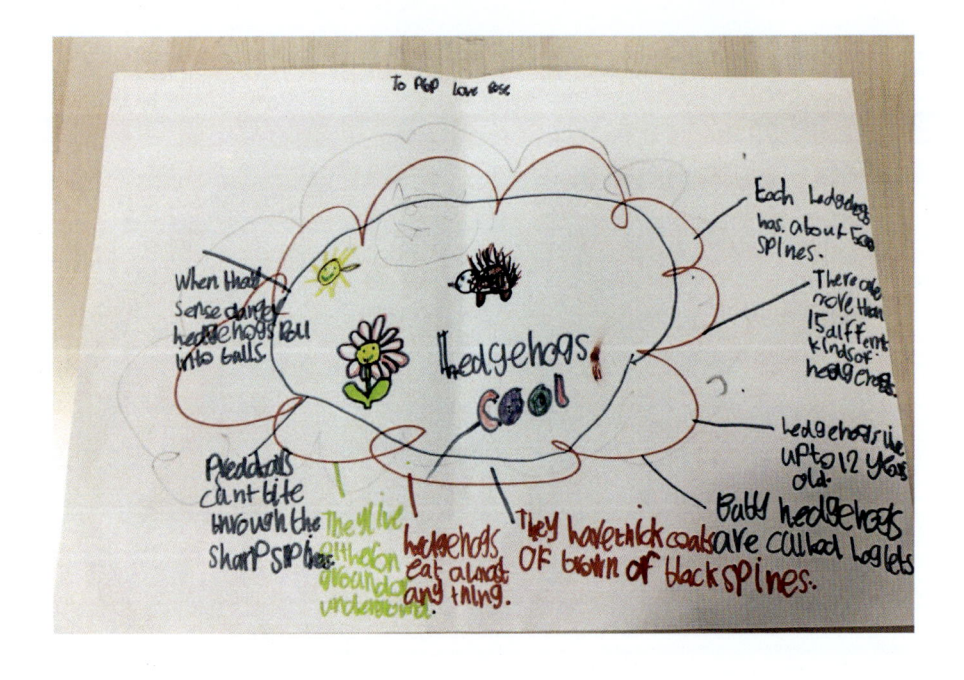

To pop love Rose

hedgehogs cool

- When that sense danger hedgehogs roll into balls.
- Each hedgehog has about 500 spines.
- There are more than 15 different kinds of hedgehogs.
- Hedgehogs live up to 12 years old.
- Predators can't bite through the sharp spines.
- They live out the on ground and underground.
- Hedgehogs eat almost anything.
- They have thick coats of brown or black spines.
- Baby hedgehogs are called hoglets.

Hedgehogs live in a nest

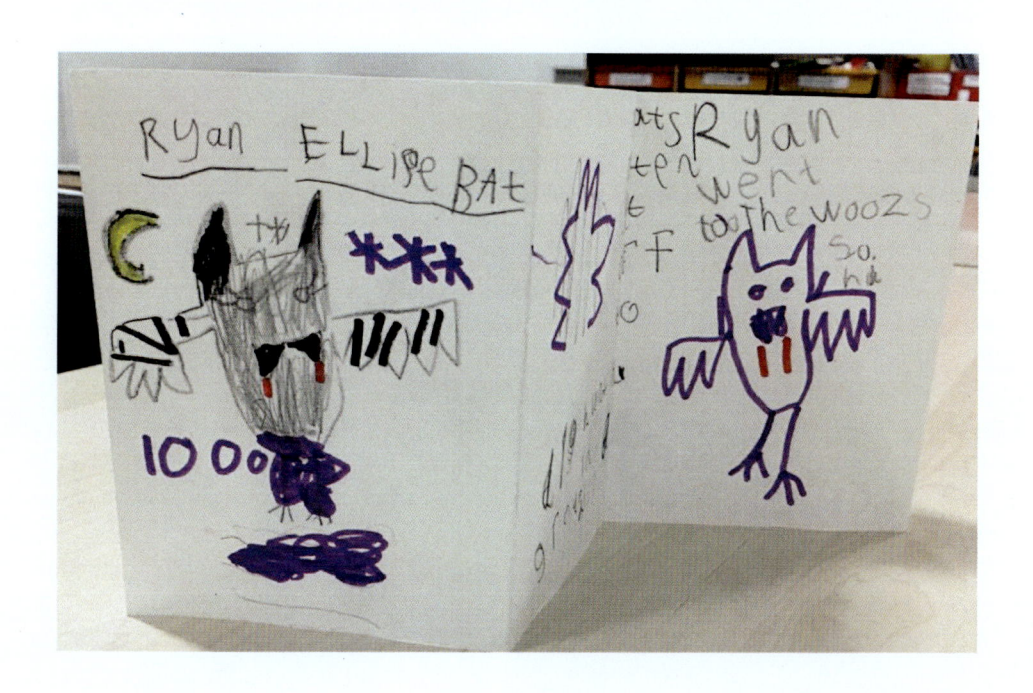

Hedgehogs look for insects and worms to eat

Night animals

Hedgehogs are awake at night. They are nocturnal animals.

fox
bat
owl
hedgehog

Ryan Ellie Bat

100

Ryan went to the woozs so he

62 Four approaches to planning a storyline

> The Tall Tree
> The Faraway Forest
> Storyland
> 17.11.16
>
> Dear Boys and Girls,
>
> I wanted to say a really big thank you for your excellent booklets and posters you made about my nocturnal friends! They were great and had so much information on them, they will definitely help in sharing who we are and what we do.
>
> Myself and my bat and hedgehog friends are so grateful for what you have done for us and hope that you can continue to share your knowledge.
>
> I therefore have one last request for you all; could you share the booklets and posters you have made with some others?
>
> Yours sincerely
>
> Plop

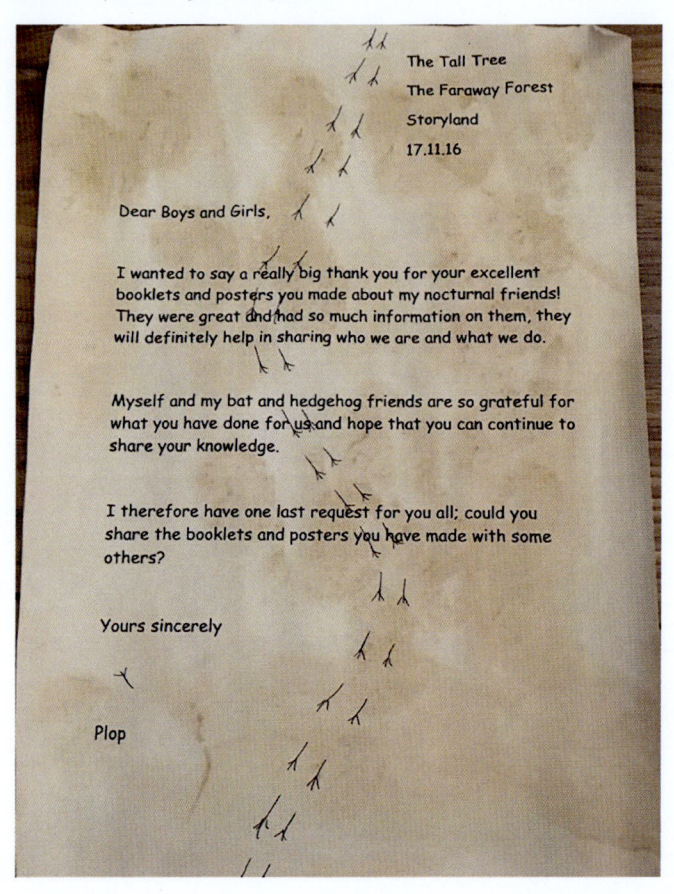

The culmination of the project was an invitation to other classes and parents to see all the work the children had done on owls and nocturnal animals.

From a pupil perspective they had responded to a cry for help from Plop. They had solved problems, researched, discussed and created. Most of all, they had had a fun adventure.

From a teacher perspective, social skills, listening and talking, reading and writing were developed in an authentic context. Researching, recording and presenting were also explored.

The storyline was truly interdisciplinary as they developed their knowledge and understanding in Social Studies as they developed their literacy skills in listening, talking and finding out information and presenting it in an interesting way.

The response from the pupils and parents was one of fun and enjoyment – learning with passion!

This was quite a short storyline with only a few episodes. With older learners, though, you could keep the interaction going with more letters and requests for information or help.

In terms of the learning it is easy to see how the literacy elements could be taught whilst at the same time other curricular elements could be developed; for example, the skills and knowledge connected with a particular topic. Science could be explored through a shared problem. History could be a focus if the novel used featured a historical character seeking their help.

As ever with Storyline, the only restriction is your imagination and the connections to the intended curricular learning.

Health and Wellbeing: positive mental health

This storyline involves a fictitious school who have got in touch to seek advice from the teacher and their class. The scenario is that the school situation is very challenging and there are often disruptions and tears.

The fictitious teacher, Hilary, has sent a letter asking for some support.

Challenging School
Somewhere far away

Dear friend,

I was wondering if you and your class could help us.

We have a challenging group of children with us this year and there always seems to be something worrying them. If it's not people falling out and feeling angry, it's somebody being sad or left out. Sometimes there are dilemmas with peer pressure and sometimes it is just that some children find it difficult to fit in and to make friends.

Anyway, I wonder if your class would be prepared to act as our support and guidance for a while. All that would be involved would be for you to allow us to send you a weekly update of some of the dilemmas causing us concern. You could discuss them in groups and then send us your ideas and strategies and we could try them out.

Of course, we would be happy to do the same for you, in return, if you need us.

Have a chat with your class and let us know what you think.

Yours faithfully,
Hilary, Wendy, Brash

The class would be invited to think of ideas to try to help. They would be asked if they ever had these problems and what strategies they had to help them.

The teacher might model some of the dilemmas described and some possible strategies to help. Initially, they might work with the class as a whole. Later each group might be more independent (though they might still share the work of each group in a plenary section of the lesson).

If and when any dilemmas, disputes or difficulties occur in the class, the teacher might suggest that the group write the dilemma down so it can be sent to the 'other school.'

A response can be penned by the teacher or by pupils in another class, or the 'dilemma' could be re-worded and given to another group in the same class so that the class 'support themselves.'

The objective is to raise awareness of mental health dilemmas and begin to feel more confident in talking about them. The groups would begin to consider different strategies and responses to help them cope in these imaginary scenarios. This would build resilience and capacity for them in their own lives in the real world.

After a few dilemma letters and responses have been exchanged with the class the next phase would be to have the class working in groups. Each day there would be different letters for each group to share and discuss and for them to form a reply.

For this topic there would be, say, six sets of 'dilemma letters' times six groups.

These could be very simple and short but would cover typical childhood mental health dilemmas (positive and negative – not just a deficit dilemmas approach).

Themes for the 'dilemma letters'

Making friends	Bullying	Peer pressure	Showing affection	Controlling anger	Feeling sad
I can't concentrate	Showing you care	How to say sorry	I'm worried about . . .	Owning up	Asking for help
She stole my friends	They won't let me play	He keeps copying	Why do I always fail?	Nobody cares	My pet died
I did a bad thing	It's not fair	They stop me concentrating	How can I help Mum?	I want time with Dad	I'm always hungry
I'm not as pretty as them	I never get picked for the team	They think I'm stupid	How do I invite Sam and Joe but not Sandy?	Everyone has a smartphone but me	My brother is always so annoying
We have to move home	I'm still scared of the dark	I'm frightened of the dentist	I don't like any food	I'm new to school	Nobody helps me with my homework

Initially the class can discuss and respond – with some help and scaffolding from the teacher and from each other. After a few 'episodes' the groups can be encouraged to send some of their own dilemmas/experiences to the other school.

Rather than respond to these, the teacher might simply recycle them (changing the names and setting, so it seems they are from the other school).

This would mean that a very pressing situation for Group A in the class could be debated and responded to by Group B (who would think it was something from the other school). Hence the children in class could help each other, from a position of security, thinking it was someone else who had the dilemma.

This kind of topic could go on for as long as the teacher felt was necessary. It could be linked to the Health and Wellbeing curriculum as well as the literacy elements of listening and talking and letter writing.

This convention of using a letter to drive the narrative has many applications. You can find more ideas for using this approach in the Appendices.

Summary

In this chapter we have looked at the convention of using a letter to drive the narrative. This can be 'dressed up' with feathers or some symbol, as in the storyline about *The Owl Who Was Afraid of the Dark*, or could perhaps arrive via the school secretary in a 'posh envelope,' or even be in an elaborate box delivered by the postman or school janitor! I have even seen the message delivered via a webcast on the smartboard – this was a video message from the class teacher's friend who had dressed up for the occasion!

The letters invite the learners to join in and suspend their disbelief, and then they get immersed in the storyline and want to help. They end up listening, talking, reading, writing and, most of all, learning with enthusiasm – with an authentic audience and purpose. The learners 'own' the learning and the direction of the narrative whilst all the teacher still holds the line that is their curricular learning.

At the end of this book you will see some other suggestions for storylines that employ the convention of a letter. Indeed, many storylines employ several devices to drive the narrative. For example, you might have introduced the WWII topic through the conventions of the family and the Street, but you might then go on to drive the narrative through letters delivered to the houses informing them of the events of the war, enlisting volunteers to the army or telling them how to build an Anderson shelter.

In the next chapter we will look at the convention of a challenge for the class to undertake – this too might be introduced or advanced through the device of a letter to be delivered, discussed and responded to.

7 The Challenge
Junior Dragons' Den and *The Apprentice* storylines

Another way to create an authentic learning context in the classroom is to create a challenge for the class. This challenge can be presented to them in a variety of ways. It could come in the form of a letter addressed to the class (see Chapter 6 for more on this convention) or it could come in the form of a visitor (see Chapter 8 for more on this). Alternatively, it could be presented in the form of a leaflet or 'flier' that is left for the children to 'find' and read – with the hope that they might come to the teacher and ask if they can enter the competition/challenge!

In this chapter we will be looking at how a challenge based on a well-known TV show might be used to advance the learning in Literacy and Technology.

Enterprise storyline: *Junior Dragons' Den*

This topic combines learning outcomes in Science and Technology and some from Social Studies.

This will involve the children exploring traditional children's games known by their families and famous in the area, as well as them being tasked with making their own games for a competition.

The hook will be a letter addressed to the class from the teachers' contact on the TV show *Dragons' Den* (see the sample letter below).

Junior Dragons' Den Auditions

1. *Junior Dragons' Den* are looking for entries on children's toys and games.
2. The Dragons want ideas to do with playground games, toys, board games and computer games.
3. You might begin by doing some market research to find out what games people know and enjoy, and what it is about them that makes them popular and successful.
4. In particular you should research local and traditional outdoor games familiar to your families and relations.

You might begin by encouraging the class to have ideas and to participate. However, you might point out that they might not actually get through to the show –nevertheless it will be fun to try. Thereafter they can be put into groups and then follow a process such as:

1   Market research – what games do we know and like?
2   What games did our parents enjoy? Why haven't they survived?
3   Why were these games popular?
4   What are the 'ingredients' of a good game?
5   Design: how do the games work? Can we investigate them in order to see how they are created and how they work?
6   What about the packaging? What about marketing?
7   Create: brainstorm ideas for our own games.

The teacher will have the line: they will have looked at the curriculum documents and ascertained the learning potential of the topic. This challenge should motivate the class to be involved and they should all have a clear sense of audience and purpose.

The class will work in groups exploring the challenge questions. This will involve listening and talking, working with the school community and some historical research. Of course, there will also be the recording of information, and the presenting skills for the 'pitch,' to work on.

It might be that another letter – or a visitor to the class – might be necessary to galvanise the class to move from the original idea to a more detailed brief: each group could work on the history of local games before looking at their own original ideas. These ideas could be trialled, polished and prepared for their 'pitch' to the Dragons. Finally, there would be a 'celebration' as they pitch their inventions to the Dragons.

The Dragons could be members of the school community, parents or local business people. The presentations could be done 'live' to these visitors or could be videoed and edited beforehand. Feedback and evaluation could come from the Dragons themselves.

It is likely that the class could easily get carried away with such a brief, so it is important for the teacher to remember that it should be all about the learning, and *not* the activities.

It is really important to guide the storyline to develop in a way that leads them to meet the learning outcomes required. Of course, the assessment evidence will be through observation of the planning discussions as well as their physical plans for their games. The final product will also be an indication of how well the learning has progressed in Literacy, History and Technology.

An alternative challenge below is for learning based on the same *Dragons' Den* theme but with its focus more on history and technology.

Dragons' Den modification for History and Technology

One modification for this creative approach is to include it in a way that links History and Technology in an interdisciplinary manner.

The class are divided into groups and a letter is delivered at the start of the day. The letter is from the Dragons.

Dear Pupils,

We are looking for an incredible invention to win the award of 'The Best Invention of the 18th Century.'

We want you to work in your groups to do some research to find out what you think was the most important invention from this time.

You will need to tell us all about the invention:

- Who was responsible?
- How was it discovered or created?
- How does it work?
- What impact did it have at the time?
- In what way did it influence what we have now?

Each group will have the opportunity to make a pitch to the Dragons to see if they can provide enough details to become the winner of 'The Best Invention of the 18th Century.' Here are some inventions to consider:

- The steam engine;
- The locomotive;
- The telephone;
- The telegraph;
- The internal combustion engine;
- The rifle;
- Ironclad ships;
- Electricity/the light bulb.

You can use any of the resources provided by your teacher as well as what you might find online. However, it is vital that you tell the Dragons where you found the information. Each fact must be linked to at least two sources to prove that it is true.

When you are ready for the presentation of your research your teacher will contact us and we will arrange to come to the school for our *Inventions Dragons' Den*.

Some of you will be invited to help with the filming of this event.

Please sign below if you are prepared to undertake this challenge.

The thinking here is that the class will do the research, find information (from more than one source) and record and present it. They will need to consider the skills and approaches to research and, in particular, ways of presenting the information in a persuasive and entertaining style.

The Dragons will be adults from the school and community: perhaps the headteacher, a parent helper, a local business person and someone in the school who might volunteer – the janitor or a member of the kitchen staff, for example. They may dress up for the occasion and some of the class will be responsible for the videoing of the event.

The video then will provide a record of the learning. It will be something that can be used as a self-assessment and peer assessment tool. It will also be invaluable as a means of sharing the learning with the parents of the pupils.

The topic might be linked to a History-based project, such as 'the Victorians,' or a Technology-based programme of work. The interdisciplinary learning can focus on outcomes in both of these subjects. Skills in research, note-taking, organising and arranging the information and recording and presenting can all be developed. There will be many links to Literacy too, with persuasive writing as a focus.

The video will provide opportunities for the development of other skills, such as providing effective feedback.

There will also be opportunities to develop social skills such as collaborative group work, organising and managing groups, sharing resources and developing presentation skills.

This approach enables the teacher to control the line. The teacher provides the sources of information. The teacher organises the groups and the timescale. It is the pupils, however, who decide which invention to explore and present. They decide how to record and organise the information. They decide how to present their learning at the end.

The teacher decides when the Dragons arrive and how to capture the learning.

Both the teacher and the pupils have the ownership of the assessment and feedback.

The whole school community can benefit from the experience – providing an audience for the presentations and helping to celebrate the product of their learning.

TV shows: *The Apprentice*

TV shows are a good source of inspiration and, like *Dragons Den*, many have a challenge element to them. Another popular programme currently being broadcast in the UK and America is *The Apprentice*. In this show there are a number of candidates working to win the title from a celebrity businessman. Each week they are involved in an enterprise challenge to see who can raise the most money. Although in the TV programme the spirit of teamwork and collaboration is not always demonstrated in the best way, you can still use the basic idea for your storyline.

The class can be divided into groups with a challenge to make the most money at the school fair. They can all be given the same brief and the same materials. The task will be to create something to sell and the winners will be the group who make the most profit.

In terms of learning the teacher can include elements in the brief to guide the learners in a particular direction. For example, a topic called 'Fair Trade' will enable the class to learn something about fair trade and its principles. The challenge might be to research and find out information for a stall at the fair. There will need to be a product to sell and it will need to contain only ingredients/materials that have been ethically sourced. Such a challenge enables learning to take place in terms of Social Studies, Technology and Enterprise. The values aspect of learning can also be developed through such an approach.

Alternatively, the challenge might be to do with healthy eating. Each group might have to challenge to create and sell the healthiest smoothie or home-baked product(s) to sell. Again, there would need to be research and a presentation of what the pupils learn.

There needs to be a sense of audience and purpose. The product would need to be labelled and marketed. The winning group would be the one who demonstrated their learning as well as selling the most!

In both of these examples there are opportunities for pupil ownership and choice. They can create the 'story.' Meanwhile, the teacher holds the line and can determine the learning focus for the class. Assessment evidence will once again come from a combination of teacher observation, examination of the products and the presentation at the end as they try to sell their goods.

Summary

In this chapter we have looked at how popular TV shows can provide the inspiration for learning. The format of the shows provides a meaningful context and in turn this creates an authentic audience and purpose for the learning. In each example there are opportunities for pupil autonomy and choice whilst at the same time the teacher can hold the line and the learning. In the above examples the emphasis is on skills and attitudes as well as in technology, enterprise and marketing. So rich is the learning potential here it will be really important to be clear what the focus will be and what it is that the teacher wants the class to learn. There will be much incidental learning going on and it could easily degenerate into a 'cross-curricular potpourri,' so careful planning is needed regarding what it is the teacher wants the class to learn and what they want to collect assessment evidence on. We will return to the challenges of the planning and assessment of a Storyline approach later on in this book.

8 The Visitor
A Visitor from Space, *The Lighthouse Keeper's Lunch* and a Rabbie Burns storyline

In this chapter we will look at the idea of using the device of a visitor to hook the children in and then to drive the narrative for the storyline. Much of the success of this will be down to how well your visitor can convince the class that they want to help. If the visitor is well prepared, they can come in and create a context for learning which has a clear audience and purpose and a definite end-point. Generally, the visitor would ask the class for help and then go away until the end of the topic, where they would return to see what the class have found out.

In this chapter we will look at using this approach for a visitor from space and one from a novel, and also a storyline about a visit from Rabbie Burns.

The Visitor

One way of establishing and developing a storyline narrative is through the convention of the Visitor. The visitor can be a real live person, often disguised appropriately (Charles Dickens, a Roman soldier, a forest fairy). The visitor will explain their context, usually including a problem to be solved: how do I get back home? How do I save my people? How can I believe what they say? Of course, they will urge the class to help them.

The visitor appears at the start of the narrative and also at the finale/celebration.

In between appearances the visitor might communicate via letter, email or video message in order to drive the narrative.

Sometimes the visitor isn't 'live' as such; a puppet might be used, or a video message, or a stuffed animal or effigy. For example, I once created a new 'pupil' for my class using old school uniform from Lost Property stuffed with newspaper and a papier mâché head. When the class came in and found the new child their curiosity led the narrative: who was this? Where did the new child live? I called the child Sandy and the class soon got to work inventing a back story, an address and a whole family. Thereafter Sandy would ask the class for help with school work or playground problems. This visitor became an active member of the class and the class were sad when one day Sandy said it was time to leave. The farewell party is well remembered to this very day!

I have seen students on placement work together so that one would dress up as a Roman soldier who is lost and confused. The class were asked to find out all about his legion and

Four approaches to planning a storyline

the events of a particular battle. The soldier needed certain information before he could travel back to his own time. Again, it was the character, the relationship and the narrative that stoked the curiosity of the children and motivated them to research, record and present what they had learned in order to help their new friend. As usual the storyline ended with a celebration before the Roman was on his way. It is this curiosity and personal engagement that brings the passion into the learning.

Below is a more detailed description of a storyline that employs the device of the visitor to drive the narrative. I have seen this done several times in Early Years classrooms.

A Visitor from Space

This is a good storyline to use for topics concerned with learning about space, the planets and the place that the Earth has in the solar system. This narrative is driven by a visitor from outer space.

This works particularly well in an Early Years classroom but has also been used successfully in a Middle Years setting.

As ever, the success of the deception depends to a large extent on the way that the teacher can 'sell' the idea to the learners. Even when they know that it is a deception, there can still be a successful experience, as long as all are willing to suspend their disbelief!

The hook

One of my students tried this with a P2 class in a challenging area of the city. She planted her 'alien' on the carpet beside an open window. She knocked a table over and scattered a few things beside it to give the impression that it had fallen to the Earth through the open window. There was even a broken 'rocket' there too.

When the class came in they exclaimed about the mess. Someone saw the character on the floor and another child found an 'emergency pod' beside it.

The class were settled down and speculated about who this character was and where it had come from. They investigated the rocket and the pod bearing the word 'Emergency.'

There was some discussion about the 'black box' carried by aircraft and then they opened the 'pod.'

Inside was this message:

> If you have found this pod it means that I must be in trouble. Please help me.
>
> I am from a hot planet in the solar system. My planet is red and has a special gas that keeps me alive. Although I cannot speak I am quite good at reading and writing. I need to get back to my planet. Can you help me to find out which way to go?
>
> It would be helpful for me if you could draw me your own planet and tell me all about it. I need to know what it looks like, what gases and liquids there are and what you like to eat and drink. Where does your food come from?

The class then discussed what they knew about space, the planets and the Earth. They worked in groups to draw pictures of the Earth (as seen from space) and these were annotated with information that they gathered from topic books and internet searches.

The learning intention was 'We are learning about what we need to survive.'

An alternative introduction to this topic used technology instead of the 'pod.' The teacher put a large silver box/bin in the middle of the classroom as a pretend spacecraft containing a letter from a friendly alien. This was surrounded by upturned chairs. Inside there was a letter that read: "We need your help. Access video message." This led to a web page featuring the alien speaking to the class.

The video message can be devised using animation software like the Talking Avatar and Facial Animation Software available online from Crazy Talk (Reallusion). This software can be useful to bring a bit more authenticity to the narrative and can be used in place of messages written on paper.

In the video clip the alien tells the class that they have been chosen to help him. He asks if the children can help: his family and friends need a new home because there is not enough space left on their own planet.

The next step in both of these approaches is to ask the class what they should do. Hopefully they will want to help the alien visitor and will do the research and develop technology skills to provide the knowledge and skills to send the alien back to its home planet.

The narrative can be driven through interaction with the alien – either through the use of letters or notes left in the classroom, or through the use of some sort of a puppet. For example, one student used a puppet of an alien. Only she could hear what 'Allie Alien' was saying, so she had to interpret and request information and suggestions from the children and relay them to Allie. Effectively, this device of the visitor enabled the narrative to be developed and the children felt that they had a lot of influence over the story whilst the teacher held the line and structured the learning intended through the things she said Allie was asking them to find out.

You can read an outline of a teacher's experience of delivering this storyline in Appendix 3. In Appendix 2 you will find another resource, an alien writing frame, which was used with this topic.

The Lighthouse Keeper's Lunch

Another approach is to have the visitor be a character from a novel that is familiar to the class and then to get the character to interact with them by leaving messages and requests in the style of the alien visitor above.

A picture book used commonly in the early years of the primary school is *The Lighthouse Keeper's Lunch* by Ronda and David Armitage (Andre Deutsch 1977). In this charming story Mr Grinling works at the lighthouse out at sea. His wife prepares his lunch every day but the seagulls keep stealing it.

Instead of reading the story to the class you could do this as a storyline using the convention of the Visitor. When I saw this done with a class of 7-year-old pupils it was the grandfather of the class teacher who pretended to be Mr Grinling. He dressed up for the part and came into the classroom one day to speak to the class. It went something like this:

Hello children,

I am your teacher Mrs Hunter's granddad. I work on a lighthouse. Who can tell me what a lighthouse is and what it is for? Anyway, every day I row the boat out to the island to go to work and every day the seagulls swoop down and steal my lunch! I have tried all sorts of things but can't seem to stop them. In desperation, I thought I would come and ask you. You look a bright lot and I know that children are usually very creative, with great imaginations. I wonder if you could come up with a solution to my problem. I know you are all busy and I need to get off to work myself, so I will leave it with you and Mrs Hunter to see what you can do.

Bye!

Thus, the stage was set. The class had a task to do. There was an audience and purpose, and the motivation to learn came from the sympathy of the class with the problem of poor Mr Grinling. Once he had left, the teacher was then able to guide the discussion and the exploring to encourage the class to use technology and problem-solving skills to create,

LI. We are learning to create a labelled diagram.

Challenge: create a diagram to show a way Mrs Grinling can get Mr Grinling's lunch to the lighthouse from the cottage.

(child's labelled drawing: Cottage, Seagull, Boat, Lighthouse)

LI. We are learning to create a labelled diagram.

Challenge: create a diagram to show a way Mrs Grinling can get Mr Grinling's lunch to the lighthouse from the cottage.

(child's labelled drawing: cottage, seagull, speed boat, cloud, pulling lunch up)

76 *Four approaches to planning a storyline*

LI. We are learning to create a labelled diagram.

Challenge: create a diagram to show a way Mrs Grinling can get Mr Grinling's lunch to the lighthouse from the cottage.

design and make possible solutions to the problem. The teacher had a clear idea of the intended learning and had already sourced a range of technology equipment, as well as general model-making materials ready for the topic. The class were keen and excited to do their best for Mr Grinling.

Over the next few days children came to Mrs Hunter with prototypes of their solution. In order to keep the pupils motivated and encourage them to test their inventions, there were letters from Mr Grinling telling them what he thought of their ideas so far.

A week later the visitor returned and asked them all to show him what they had come up with. Each group presented to him their plan and their solution. They had to explain their ideas and justify the materials and approaches taken. Finally, he chose a couple of their ideas to take away to try in 'real life,' with a promise to let them know how he got on. In the meantime he invited them to the dining hall to join him for a school lunch (fish fingers, of course!).

This short topic is a good example of how you might use a character to promote the storyline theme. The class are invited to believe that the character has really come from the book, and after that the narrative can be driven in a way that advances the learning. Clearly in this topic there was a lot of assessment evidence produced in their drawings and models. Formative feedback was provided via the letters exchanged as the class worked on prototypes during the week that Mr Grinling was away.

The third example of using a visitor to drive the narrative is to have a visit from someone famous.

Rabbie Burns

In this storyline the visitor appeared in the classroom dressed as Robert Burns, the famous Scottish poet. The children were excited and were asked if they knew who he was. Once it was established that this was the Bard of Ayrshire himself, there was discussion about his life and works. Pupils were asked what they knew about him and if they knew any of his poems. Rabbie then asked them for help:

> What I need, boys and girls, is for you to help me. Last week I had a bump on the head and I can't remember much at all about myself. Perhaps you could find out some things to remind me of where I was born, where I lived and what it was that made me so famous. I have heard of something called a 'Burns supper,' and I wonder if you could show me what this is all about. I am needing to go away for a wee lie down now but I promise to come back soon to see how you all got on.
> Bye!

Thus, the scene was set and the challenge issued. The class, though a little dubious as to the real identity of this man, were nevertheless keen to help him out with his amnesia:

- They set about looking for information and discussing the best way to record and present this to him. They also began to look at his poems.
- Some work was done on analysing why they did (and did not) like his poems.
- 'The Selkirk Grace,' 'Address to a Haggis' and 'The Immortal Memory' were explored and memorised as a group ready for the Burns supper.
- Next the class had to research the traditions of the Burns supper.
- One group explored what to wear, another what to eat and yet another what to say – in terms of the poems relating to the occasion.
- Finally, a group looked at the running order and a master of ceremonies was established.

A few weeks later, much work had been done on creating costumes, writing to the local butchers and supermarkets and sourcing the 'feast' for the big occasion. Parents were invited to hear all about Rabbie Burns, and to take part in the festivities. Of course, the Bard himself took centre stage and even recited some of his best-known poems.

In terms of the learning, the class covered a good deal of their Literacy outcomes. They explored the poems through much listening and talking and then went on to create poems of their own. In terms of research skills there were opportunities to develop skills in note taking, researching, recording and presenting. In terms of History or social subjects there was all of the research into the life of Burns, including discussion regarding reliable sources and consulting books, songs and paintings as well as the online resources about the life of the poet.

One of the things that made this a success was the fact that the visitor managed to establish a relationship with the class on that first visit. A relationship that prompted them to, once again, suspend their disbelief and put in the learning effort to help someone out.

Clearly this device of a famous visitor who has conveniently lost their memory can apply to lots of learning situations. It could be Van Gogh needing information about his life and work. Or it could be Julius Caesar needing vital information about his empire.

The success, of course, is down to doing a convincing job at the start and having a visitor who is convincing enough to persuade the class to enter into the fantasy and to want to do their best for the sake of the story. Each of these ideas would involve some sort of celebration: a performance, a party, an exhibition or a solution to a problem. For each of these there would be a line held by the teacher to ensure that the learning takes place – but for them all it will be the children themselves that create and maintain the story that carries the narrative.

Summary

In this chapter we have explored how having a visitor to the class can establish a context, an audience and a purpose for learning. The visitor can be a real person, living or dead, like Rabbie Burns. They can be a character from a book like *The Lighthouse Keeper's Lunch*, or it can be a puppet like the alien visitor seeking help. As long as the teacher has thought through the curricular elements of the learning and the visitor is well prepped, the class should find themselves immersed in the learning context and looking forward to the end-of-story celebrations where they can share what they have learned with their visitor.

At the end of this book you will find some other ideas for using a visitor in this way.

Part III
Assessment and planning approaches

9 Choosing your Storyline approach

In this chapter we will be considering the process of deciding which Storyline approach to use. So far we have explored the basic concept of using Storyline to promote a passion for learning in an interdisciplinary way. We have also looked at four possible approaches:

- the Street;
- the Letter;
- the Challenge;
- the Visitor.

In this chapter we will use the theme of the rainforest and analyse how each of these approaches might be used in order to grab the attention of the learners and to carry the narrative for their learning.

First, a reminder of the planning process:

1. Choose the context.
2. Decide on the learning *focus*.
3. Decide on the *kind* of storyline.
4. Decide on a *way in* (the hook).
5. Think about the *progression through the topic*.
6. Focus on the *learning*, the key questions, the skills, knowledge and attitudes.
7. Plan for normal life, its tasks, celebrations, rituals and routines.
8. Plan the *special event*, celebration, turning point or climax to end the narrative.
9. Think about how you will facilitate the *reflection and evaluation* of the story and the learning that has taken place.
10. Consider what *evidence* you might have at the end of the topic to show the learning that has taken place.

Let us look at this in a little more detail.

Choose the context

I have chosen 'the rainforest' as it is a staple project used in primary schools throughout the world. It provides pupils with the opportunity to explore and learn about other cultures, wildlife and people. It provides them with an insight to the way our planet is used, for good and bad. It also highlights global issues such as deforestation, fair trade and the impact man can have on the environment.

Decide on the learning *focus*

There is so much learning that might take place in a topic on the rainforest. The best way to approach this would be to look at the curriculum guidelines provided by your local authority or government and basically look for ways of implementing the kind of learning prescribed.

Some critics of the interdisciplinary approach say that there is not the flexibility any more for teacher autonomy. In England there is a lot of advice and attention on just what to teach. Yet this doesn't mean that teachers cannot take something like Storyline and use it as the vehicle for the implementation of the prescribed curriculum. In Scotland there appears to be more flexibility in terms of curricular guidance – however, there is still a requirement for a certain body of learning to take place. Wherever you teach there will be some expectation to cover key areas such as Literacy, Social Studies and environmental education. These curricular areas may have different titles in different countries but teachers will recognise them as variants on the traditional subjects: English, Geography, History and Science.

In any rainforest topic the teacher will be hoping to cover learning in terms of *where* the rainforests of the world can be found. They will want pupils to know *what* we mean by the term 'rainforest.' Some consideration will be required for the research into *who* lives in the rainforest and to *how* the situation in the rainforest can have an impact on their lives. Above all, we want the pupils to learn how they can make a positive difference to the rainforest and to their world and *why* this all matters.

Experienced teachers will recognise this approach to interpreting the curriculum.

The basic questions *who, what, why, when, where* and *how* all provide a starting point and structure to the learning.

Teacher research

So, we begin with a bit of teacher research. This may include reading up on some basic information about the subject. It may also involve looking at resources already available in the school. In some cases it may involve looking at the 'off the shelf' topic in the school – the one that has perhaps been used over and over again in the same way for years.

These starting points should enable the planning to be done in an informed way. This is the meat of the project – the storyline will be the all-important skeleton on which we hang all of this learning.

Of course, we could easily plan to cover a number of curricular areas from Art and Geography to Science, Biology and RE. The trouble with this is that if we introduce too many curricular areas we just provide a very superficial experience for the learner. Therefore, it is best to focus on two or three curricular areas so that you can look at the curricular guide for depth in the learning.

A good rule of thumb is to ask yourself, "What are they learning in this curricular area?" and "How will I know that the learning has taken place?"

Evidence of learning is all-important if you are to justify taking the Storyline approach.

What kind of learning?

We also need to consider what learning must encompass, so that we can plan to build in some teaching and assessment of the different elements. We need to consider elements such as:

- the product;
- the process and social skills;
- knowledge;
- learning skills;
- attitudes.

The product

Clearly the 'product' element of learning and assessment is something that teachers use every day to monitor learning progress. From marking the jotters to assessing their artwork, the 'examination of product' is perhaps the easiest way to track learning. In addition to this, however, we need to look at the actual 'process.'

The process and social skills

The process is the steps taken on the way to the product. The listening and talking, the negotiating and problem solving, the interactions and ability to overcome challenges and setbacks – all of these feature in the process of learning. For the teacher this is a little bit more difficult to evidence, but as you will see in the next chapter there are ways to support the way the teacher conducts observations and monitors this process, and Storyline provides many opportunities for the teacher to do this in an unobtrusive manner.

Knowledge

Although Storyline is essentially an immersive experience it is still something that should provide the learner with knowledge. The culminating chapter in any storyline is the celebration, which may take the form of a party, an exhibition or presentation. These celebrations provide the opportunity for the knowledge gained through the storyline to be presented in a way that makes assessment of learning crystal clear.

Learning skills

The assessment of the skills involved comes through examination of both the process and the product. Observations of how the groups go about their research tasks and the way that they present their learning will reveal much about their competency with the skills involved in the storyline tasks.

Attitudes

Many Storyline narratives provide an opportunity to explore the attitudes of the learners. When the children create their families and write about the relationships within these families they are projecting some of their own values. It might be that a child uses the family set-up to create the ideal family that he has never had. Or it might be that the child who portrays the family as always arguing is really expressing some of his or her own family issues. A topic on fair trade or refugees might also expose some of the attitudes and prejudices in the learners and provide opportunities to explore different perspectives and points of view.

Storyline, then, provides an opportunity to consider all of these elements in terms of our learning objectives. There is more detailed information on assessment in Chapter 11.

A rainforest storyline and the curriculum (in England)

Looking at the English curriculum requirements it is clear that a project on the rainforest can provide a good deal of learning opportunities in subjects such as Literacy, Geography and Science. See below for a summary of these learning opportunities.

English National Curriculum: Geography, Science and English Year 6

Geography	Identify the position and significance of the rainforests
	Understand geographical similarities and differences between the UK and a region in North or South America
	Describe and understand key aspects of physical geography, and human geography, including: types of settlement and land use, economic activity including trade links
	Use maps, atlases, globes and digital/computer mapping to locate countries and describe features studied
Science	Living things and their habitats: describe how living things are classified into broad groups
English	Building a varied and rich vocabulary and an increasing range of sentence structures, organising paragraphs around a theme in narratives, creating settings, characters and plot
	Read their own writing aloud, to a group or the whole class, using appropriate intonation and controlling the tone and volume so that the meaning is clear

An example of a storyline plan meeting some of the Outcomes and Experiences for the curriculum in Scotland might focus on similar learning intentions.

Scottish Curriculum for Excellence Second Level: Language and Social Studies

Listening and talking	To persuade, argue, explore using supporting detail and evidence
	I can *consider the advantages and disadvantages* and *discuss* the impact. I can compare and explain
Social studies	Comparing their own country and culture with another one. looking at advantages and disadvantages
	I can *explain* how the physical environment influences the ways in which people use land by *comparing* my local area with a contrasting area

Incidental learning	Artwork and classroom displays that go with it
There is so much scope to produce stunning work; on the forest itself, the wildlife and the sheer scale of the rainforest
Knowledge and skills	Research, recording and presenting and the comparing of cultures will be the main focus

An interpretation of the way the outcomes above might be translated into a storyline are outlined below:

Unit overview: 'the Rainforest'

The children will learn about

- what rainforests are and where in the world they can be located;
- the rainforest itself, including climates, weather and the four different layers;
- deforestation and its impacts on people and places;
- different plant and animal life that can be found in the rainforest and also about people that live there.

This work will link closely to the topic of 'habitats' within Science. Links will also be made to Literacy through 'Stories from Other Cultures.'

Work will be included on fair trade.

The curricular focus will be on Science, Geography and English. There will be some incidental learning in Art and Biology.

Key objectives

1. To ask geographical questions; for example, "What is this landscape like?" and "What do I think about it?"
2. To use secondary sources of information, including photographs, for example; stories; information texts; the internet; satellite images; videos and artefacts.
3. To produce different genres of writing:
    a. composition: imaginative writing;
    b. newspaper articles;
    c. non-fiction text: fact files;
    d. persuasive writing.
4. To identify and describe
    a. what places are like; for example, in terms of weather and jobs;
    b. the location of places and environments they study;
    c. where places are; for example, in which region/country the places are, whether they are near rivers or hills and what the nearest towns or cities are;

(continued)

86 Assessment and planning approaches

(continued)

    d why places are like they are; for example, in terms of weather conditions, local resources and historical development;

    e how and why places change – for example, through deforestation and conservation projects – and how they may change in the future; for example, through an influx of tourists.

5 Success criteria: must be able to name

    a a rainforest and some of its different layers;
    b plants and animals that live there and why this is a suitable habitat for them;
    c rainforests, and locate them on a globe or map.

6 They can talk about

    a the climate and how plants/animals are suited to their habitat;
    b deforestation and how this can impact upon people and places;
    c how fair-trade farming can help support workers in the rainforest.

7 Some children will be able to

    a name and locate rainforests on a globe or map;
    b suggest how a plant or animal has adapted to its environment;
    c talk about deforestation in terms of primary and secondary impacts.

Decide on the *kind* of storyline

Having established a clear idea of the learning potential and narrowed this to a few specific learning intentions it is time to think about the best way to introduce a narrative to hang this on. We might consider each of the four approaches in turn.

The Street

At first sight you might not feel that this would be believable, but it rather depends on how you want to approach this. For example, you might create a context where the 'families' are going on a trip to the rainforest and when they get there they will stay in a 'village.' This village will provide the 'street,' yet it could be a row of tents as they go on a camping holiday for the storyline. Alternatively, it could be that you ask them to research the kind of homes that the people who live in the rainforest are likely to have. This research will enable them to create houses. It will also get them interested in other aspects of like in the rainforest. Another possibility is that they 'live' in a street on the fringes of the rainforest.

    Whichever version you choose you can then develop your narrative along the usual lines:

- families;
- homes;

- everyday life;
- an incident;
- a resolution/celebration.

But first let us look at the other possibilities for our narrative.

The Letter

Another way in would be for the class to receive a letter. This might simply be a letter allegedly from some of the villagers who live on the fringes of the rainforest seeking 'pen pals' or requesting support with an important environmental issue.

The narrative may well begin with the pen pals writing to tell pupils about their families and homes and then asking your class to do the same.

They could also tell pupils about normal day-to-day life until the 'incident' happens.

Such an incident might be the threat of further deforestation and involve the arguments for and against this.

Clearly this would enable much of the learning outlined in the plans above to be delivered.

The Challenge

There are various ways that the rainforest project could be approached via a challenge.

It could be linked to the visitor ideas below: the visitor could speak about 'normal life' and then go on to tell the class about some of the challenges facing the people or animals of the rainforest. The class could then be asked to help in some way, perhaps looking for a solution to save an endangered species or plant.

Another approach would be to make the project itself a challenge. The class could be asked to research, record and present information on different elements of the rainforest: the emergent layer, the canopy, the understorey or the forest floor, for example.

This in itself is not a narrative way of learning but could provide the initial background information prior to the teacher introducing the narrative element.

The teacher could ask them to pretend that they have crash-landed in the rainforest and now need to survive until help comes. The storyline could have different episodes within which there are challenges to be solved: where to get water or how to hide from snakes, for example. Eventually they could meet the indigenous people of the forest. Thereafter they could be called upon to help the people to try to stop further deforestation.

Again, the evidence of learning might be the presentation of ideas and understanding. It might be letters the pupils write or a drama showing what they would do and say if they were in the real-life situation.

The Visitor

To pull this off one needs a friend who is happy to dress up and assume the identity of a person who lives in the rainforest. Alternatively, they could take on the role of an 'expert' from the rainforest region.

The class would be given some background before the visit:

Teacher: Someone is coming to speak to us about the rainforest. Before the visit we need to look into what we mean by 'the rainforest.' We need to know something about what it is like, who lives there and what use the people make of the land, et cetera.

On the day of the visit the visitor can develop this initial knowledge but also add more information. They might then introduce the 'incident' in the guise of a problem to be solved. Again, the debate about deforestation and its impact on the people and animals of the rainforest is perfect for this part of the topic.

The class could be left with the task of finding out more and presenting some kind of argument. The visitor would return at some point to hear what the class can come up with.

What they say and produce will provide effective assessment evidence of their learning about the rainforest.

Combined approaches

It is clear that although the four main narrative approaches were introduced in the preceding chapters as being separate and distinct, they can in fact be combined.

The idea of a letter and a visitor as suggested above works very well and enables dialogue and developments to move the story along through letters and visits.

The combination of a visitor or letter and a challenge also works well.

The notion of a street – in its broadest sense of someone's home – is one that will prevail through most Storyline narratives, and this is also true of the family.

The *way in* or the 'hook'

Once the approach is decided upon, the next important planning decision is to decide the best way in, or the 'hook.'

For a storyline with a letter or visitor this is easy enough. The main challenge is doing it in a way that the class can handle. They are required to suspend their disbelief in order to pretend that the narrative is not only true, but personal to them.

Narratives that begin with a family and a home succeed because the pupils have some ownership of who they are and where they live. Taking time with the first few episodes so that the pupils really 'own' their characters pays dividends later on when you challenge them to 'live in the shoes of others' once you arrive in the rainforest.

In the Appendices there is a detailed plan where the hook involves the class establishing families who then 'win' a holiday in the tropical rainforest. However, when they get there they find nowhere to stay. The cut down a few trees to make huts and that is when the trouble begins. Soon afterwards there is a visit from a representative of Conservation International, and she is not very happy with them!

Think about the progression through the topic

Once you have decided on your Storyline approach and the hook, you can think about how the tale will progress. Keep the learning intentions clear in the plan but try to involve the pupils and take their interests into account. The most important things are their interests and the learning. However, it is generally quite easy to steer their interests towards the intended learning. In this chapter, and elsewhere in the book, you will see some ideas for how you might progress a storyline topic.

Once you have decided on your Storyline approach and the hook, you can think about how the tale will progress. Keep the learning intentions clear in the plan but try to involve the pupils and take into account their interests. The most important things are their interests and the learning. However, it is generally quite easy to steer their interests towards the intended learning.

Focus on the learning

In the examples above I have tried to suggest what this progression through the topics might look like. The incident is a crucial element of the narrative. It provides the challenge and the motivation to learn and to present what they learn. Again, I have suggested some ideas about this above. Most of all, it is important to keep thinking about the key questions:

- What are they learning?
- How do we know?

It would be easy to get distracted by lots of fun activities like art, drama and writing. However, the teacher should hold the line for Storyline: keep a focus on the learning intentions and be clear on the purpose of these activities. It should be about what they learn, not what they do.

Plan for normal life, its tasks, celebrations, rituals and routines

For most storylines there needs to be some sense of everyday life before some incident or problem is introduced. In terms of the curriculum this is where the learners get to explore the difference between life for ordinary folk then compared with now. It is useful to ask them to consider key questions like: where do you live? Where do you get your food? What jobs are there? What do you do for entertainment? What religions are there? What about school and education?

Only when the learners have properly explored all of this 'everyday life' can you introduce the new neighbours, or the big land developer or the earthquake, and really challenge them into realising what will be lost when things change.

We need to plan so that there is scope and support for finding out about everyday life in the relevant time. This might mean, as the teacher, researching and sharing websites and links to useful information. It might mean scaffolding the learners so that they consider the key questions above – this might mean making worksheets or writing frames for them. As you will see elsewhere in this book oral work and drama lend themselves to this imagining and sharing what we feel it would be like living in that time in that place.

Plan the special event, celebration, turning point or climax to end the narrative

Of course, there needs to be an end-point to the topic. A celebration or action is usually planned. This might be freedom for the villages as the truckers with their deforestation plans leave with their tails between their legs. Alternatively, you might end with some sort of display sale with fair trade being the main focus. Pupils can show parents how fair trade can save much of the rainforest. Thus, the pupils can see how they have agency to affect change in their world. It is also worthwhile thinking about how the celebration might provide you with assessment evidence at the end of the topic (see the next chapter for more on this). It is a good idea to have a clear idea of the end-point right at the start of your planning so that you can build in the kind of learning and activities that will take the class to that destination.

Think about how you will facilitate the reflection and evaluation of the story and the learning that has taken place

As explained earlier in this book it is important to have a session where you and the class reflect on what you learned, and how you learned through this narrative experience. This metacognition is important so that the class see past all the fun and the activities they have been enjoying and realise the learning they have been doing: both the unique learning and the transferrable.

Consider what evidence you might have at the end of the topic to show the learning that has taken place

Finally, it is important to establish and record the learning that has taken place: most of this should be planned learning but there will of course be much incidental learning if you were successful in getting the class on board and allowing them to 'own' the story (despite the teacher holding the line!). Essentially there should be some evidence of the learning as set out in your plan. Thinking about things the learners write, say, make and do is a good approach. You will read more about this when we consider ways of assessing and presenting the learning in Chapter 11.

Summary

In this chapter we have looked at the process of planning a Storyline theme and deciding which approach to take. The decisions regarding the approach and the hook were explored. We concluded that it is sometimes possible to combine approaches and so use, for example, the Visitor and the Letter to advance the narrative.

In a topic like 'the rainforest' there is a lot of learning potential and the curriculum guidelines provide a good starting point when planning the topic.

In this chapter we investigated how a narrative might enable the delivery of the appropriate learning outcomes whilst using an inspiring narrative approach where the pupils still feel that they have some ownership of the story and of the learning.

The key principles of keeping in mind the important questions "What are they learning?", "How do we know?" and "What is the evidence of learning?" were adhered to so that learning is always at the heart of any storyline.

You can find a full rainforest storyline plan in the Appendices.

In the next chapter we will look in much more detail about how we can plan for the learning when taking a Storyline narrative approach.

10 Storyline and curriculum planning

There are many ways to plan an interdisciplinary topic.
We are going to focus on a few of them.

Start with inspiration!

You might begin with a brilliant idea and brainstorm all your ideas before going to your curriculum documents and finding where you might find permission to implement them.

For example, I might notice that the pupils in my Early Years class are keen to keep returning to the block play each day but they never go beyond trying to build the highest tower.

In order to extend and develop their play I might have an idea to use a Storyline approach.

I might have a new puppet or cuddly toy and a letter as the driving force behind our narrative. Perhaps the puppet could be a farmer. The farmer can leave a letter saying he needs somewhere to keep his cows, sheep, ducks and chickens separate but safe. The children are then invited to create a solution to this problem.

What about the curriculum?

Thus, I have a brilliant idea! But what about the curriculum?

Next, I need to go to the curriculum documents and find out why I should be directing play in this way. Is there an outcome or experience that links to this idea? I cannot go on and show how this links specifically to the current curriculum in every country where this book might be read, but I will show below how the curriculum in England and in Scotland might be delivered through a Storyline topic. Wherever you happen to teach I believe that your curriculum will not be so radically different that these ideas cannot be transferred to your curriculum guide. In any case, as the curriculum changes so often it is important to appreciate that fundamentally we all need to teach similar ideas, skills, knowledge and concepts and to acknowledge that Storyline is a good way of achieving this.

Therefore, if you have a particularly good idea, like the block play one mentioned above, it is likely that the learning can be covered through a Storyline approach. Whether or not this comes under Play, Literacy, Health and Wellbeing or Social Studies, there will be outcomes and experiences that will connect to the basic idea. Later we will look in more detail at how the some of the Upper Primary curriculum outcomes might be delivered through a storyline on the rainforest.

Evidence and assessment

If you can find these links to the curriculum then the next step would be, "Will I be able to evidence the learning that takes place? How will I assess this?" It is important that we do have a clear understanding of what it is we want the pupils to gain from the experience and are able to provide evidence later to prove that we have been able to take their learning forward. So, for the example above this might require observation or some sort of a record, like a photograph. It might mean having a discussion with them afterwards where they explain what they did and why they did it. For an Upper Years class doing 'the Rainforest,' for example, it might mean that the evidence is in the pieces of writing that they do, or the video/drama that they make or the maps and inventions that they come up with.

Inspiring storyline

In an extended storyline like 'the Rainforest' or the 'WWII, My Street' approach there will be many different ways of inspiring the class. Elsewhere in this book we look at the planning process where you need to consider which Storyline approach you might take and what kind of 'hook' you might use to get things started.

Then there are the pupils, who will in turn suggest ideas that further develop the storyline. They will hold the story in this way – developing the initial ideas and taking them on, personalising and interacting and developing learning as they go. However, it is the teacher who will hold the line. The teacher will plan to implement the selected outcomes from the curriculum and make sure that the pupils' ideas lead to the required learning.

Always, the teacher will have the key assessment questions in mind as the storyline unfolds: "What are they learning? How do I know? Will I be able to evidence this learning? How will I assess this?"

Incidental learning

Of course, there will also be unplanned, incidental learning. This learning can be evaluated, recorded and assessed later, and also included in the learning profiles for the class.

If the storyline is to be successful, the pupils must have a good degree of ownership of it. Therefore, it is inevitable that there will be this unplanned learning. This is no bad thing as long as this can be noted, assessed and entered into the overall storyline plan retrospectively.

This approach, where the teacher comes up with the initial idea and finds justification in the curriculum, before setting out with a narrative that allows for pupil choice and involvement that produces further unplanned learning, is one of the many benefits of the Storyline approach.

Start with the requirements of the curriculum

Another approach might be to look at things the other way round: to begin with the curriculum guidelines. It may be that there is some cumulative record of areas of learning required to be covered by the class. The teacher may look at this and see gaps in areas of knowledge, understanding or experience that need to be filled.

For example, the class may have done a lot of history-based projects in the past but very little on 'the Earth and Space.' If that were the case the teacher might start by looking at what it is the children are meant to know and do at this stage in their primary school.

It might be that they need to know about the structure of the Earth and something about the planets in the solar system. Having identified some of the learning, the teacher can then begin to think about a suitable storyline and hook to motivate the learners. Perhaps the 'alien visitor' we met in Chapter 8.

Such a storyline could be developed and pursued safe in the knowledge that the teacher was clear about what it was the class needed to cover. As the storyline unfolds the pupils can develop the story whilst the teacher ensures that the direction of the narrative enables the learning intentions to be covered. The evidence of the learning might be the product of the pupils' work. Perhaps a map of the solar system for their alien friend, or details of each planet and their atmosphere to help in resettlement. The most important thing is that the teacher was able to look at what learning was required and then make a storyline tailor-made to provide a context, a purpose, in which the class could 'learn with passion.'

Topic headings set by the school or authority

It might be that in your context there are certain topics to be covered. For example, in Scotland many primary schools cover 'the Romans,' 'the Vikings,' 'Space' and 'Natural Disasters,' to name just a few. This might be the starting point. It is likely that the school already has resources for each prescribed topic. These can still be useful. The difference here is that you would look at the learning required by the topic and think of a good hook and context to deliver the learning. In this book we have looked at many different ways into a narrative. It might require a mystery letter from a stranded alien to get the Space topic under way. Or it might be a strange visit from the 'bank manager' asking for ideas for the Enterprise project to get started. It might be the creation of the family and the street that inspires an interest in the Battle of Hastings or the Battle of Culloden. The important thing is that the learning is identified first, then the hook and the storyline follows. The plan can still incorporate the interests and ideas of the pupils – providing ownership and relevance.

It is a good idea for pupils have several opportunities to be involved in a Storyline approach during their primary school experience. There are some schools in Scotland where each class has a storyline every single year!

Consult the class

Another common way to begin the learning is to introduce the desired learning and then to ask the pupils, "What do you know? What do you want to know? How will you find out?"

However, even this pupil-centred approach can lead to a narrative. As long as the teacher gathers the information from the class about where their interests lie, they can go on to look at the different narrative approaches suggested in this book. If, for example, the class want to learn about volcanoes, the storyline might follow a theme with families living on the slopes of a supposedly extinct volcano. From there you might look at the physical geography and the factors concerned with living in such a place. Alternatively, you might invite in an 'expert' to explain what is going on inside the volcano and how likely it is that it might erupt.

Again, if the class want to learn about fashion or movies, the Challenge approach might be employed. For example, the class might be challenged to come up with designs for a school fashion show which will be filmed and edited by them! Alternatively, a letter might arrive inviting the pupils to enter designs for a show taking place elsewhere.

Once you have experience of the four basic narrative approaches outlined in this book you will be well equipped to create your own bespoke storylines based upon the needs and interests of the pupils in your care. As outlined above, the links to the curriculum and assessment procedures will be a key component of your planning. All of these ideas allow for and indeed encourage pupil voice and ownership of the learning. Above all, the immersive nature of the narrative makes the learning exciting and fun – with that, the learning with passion can truly begin!

More detailed curriculum planning

'The Rainforest' is a popular topic in the primary school, so let us look at how we might plan for curriculum delivery through such a topic.

Below are the some of the Year 6 curriculum requirements for the curriculum in England. After each section you will find some suggestions that might enable you to deliver these through a storyline on the rainforest.

Geography KS2

Ge2/1.1 Locational Knowledge:

Identify the position and significance of latitude, longitude, Equator, Northern Hemisphere, Southern Hemisphere, the Tropics of Cancer and Capricorn, Arctic and Antarctic Circle, the Prime/Greenwich Meridian and time zones

- Storyline activities can be devised that encourage and enable pupils to establish exactly where in the world their story takes place, e.g. the Southern Hemisphere, South America

Ge2/1.2a Place Knowledge:

Understand geographical similarities and differences through the study of human and physical geography of a region of the United Kingdom, a region in a European country, and a region in North or South America

- Storyline activities can be devised that encourage pupils to make comparisons between their home and the rainforest, including landscape, wildlife and land use

---

(continued)

(continued)

Ge2/1.3a Human and Physical Geography:

Describe and understand key aspects of physical geography, including: climate zones, biomes and vegetation belts, rivers, mountains, volcanoes and earthquakes, and the water cycle

Ge2/1.3b

Describe and understand key aspects of human geography, including: types of settlement and land use, economic activity including trade links, and the distribution of natural resources including energy, food, minerals and water

- In exploring 'daily life' in the storyline pupils will understand aspects of climate, geography, land use, the economy and the use of rainforest resources
- Trade and over-development will also be explored

Ge2/1.4a Geographical Skills and Fieldwork:

Use maps, atlases, globes and digital/computer mapping to locate countries and describe features studied

Ge2/1.4c

Use fieldwork to observe, measure, record and present the human and physical features in the local area using a range of methods, including sketch maps, plans and graphs, and digital technologies

- Within the context of learning about the rainforest, pupils can be encouraged to use a range of resources to locate the country and situation of the rainforest
- They can make sketch maps of their imaginary village and plan geographical solutions to the deforestation problems that they learn about

Science KS2

Sc6/2.1a Living Things and Their Habitats:

Describe how living things are classified into broad groups according to common observable characteristics and based on similarities and differences, including micro-organisms, plants and animals

- Pupils will research and report on the wide variety of wildlife living in the four layers of the rainforest as part of their Storyline investigations
- Habitat, food chains, adaptation, etc., will also be explored and their findings will be recorded and presented

English

En3/3.3b Draft and Write:

  i composing and rehearsing sentences orally (including dialogue), progressively building a varied and rich vocabulary and an increasing range of sentence structures
  ii organising paragraphs around a theme
  iii in narratives, creating settings, characters and plot
  iv in non-narrative material, using simple organisational devices

- In a Storyline project pupils will have an audience and purpose for many different genres of writing. This will provide a context for the skills detailed above
- They will create their own characters (families) and settings (rainforest homes)
- They will provide both fiction and non-fiction texts – recording and presenting the facts that they have researched on this topic

En3/3.3e Proofread:

Read their own writing aloud, to a group or the whole class, using appropriate intonation and controlling the tone and volume so that the meaning is clear

- Pupils will prepare, proofread and present their learning in the celebration at the end of the project, either as a debate or a presentation to an audience of their peers or their parents

Similarly, in Scotland the Curriculum for Excellence provides justification for taking a Storyline approach to deliver experiences and outcomes in Social Studies and Literacy:

Social Studies Level 2
I can explain how the physical environment influences the ways in which people use land by comparing my local area with a contrasting area. SOC 2-13a
By comparing the lifestyle and culture of citizens in another country with those of Scotland, I can discuss the similarities and differences. SOC 2-19a
I can explain how the physical environment influences the ways in which people use land by comparing my local area with a contrasting area. SOC 2-13a
I can consider the advantages and disadvantages of a proposed land use development and discuss the impact this may have on the community. SOC 2-08b

Literacy Level 2
I can persuade, argue, explore issues or express an opinion using relevant supporting detail and/or evidence. LIT 2-29a
When I engage with others, I can respond in ways appropriate to my role, show that I value others' contributions and use these to build on thinking. LIT 2-02a
I can persuade, argue, explore issues or express an opinion using relevant supporting detail and/or evidence. LIT 2-29a

Listening and talking

As you can see in the outcomes above there is an emphasis on some of the skills involved in listening and talking:

> To be able to persuade, argue, explore using supporting detail and evidence. To consider the advantages and disadvantages of an argument and to be able to compare and explain.

All of these skills might be tricky to develop outside of a meaningful context. The Storyline approach provides such a context. The storyline provides both an audience and a purpose for listening, talking, reading and writing, so that the learners want to explore, compare, explain and argue for their families in the narrative. The emotional involvement that we want to create for them will be the thing that motivates and inspires them to learn in this curricular area.

Social Studies

In the outcomes for Social Studies there is also an emphasis on comparing their own country and culture with another one. Comparing and contrasting, and looking at advantages and disadvantages, are all skills that can be developed through taking a narrative approach. This may well include some work in reading for information and note taking, organising and presenting information. To some extent the focus for such a topic depends on the interests of the pupils and the teacher, or on the extent to which the curricular objectives are mapped out for the class.

Other considerations might be what has gone before. It is helpful when doing any kind of comparing and contrasting on a cultural level to have recently taken a look at your own culture. So, if the class have recently looked at their own local landscape, agriculture and general culture then the comparison work on the rainforest will mean more to them.

Knowledge, skills and attitudes

In my experience the most exciting elements of any rainforest project are the excitement and wonder the children have when they learn about the wildlife that lives there and the many products that we get from the rainforest. This might enable the 'knowledge' element of the curriculum to be fully explored. However, for the purposes of this example it is useful to consider a focus which is more concerned with skills and attitudes. So it might be that the comparing of cultures is the thing that we focus upon for assessment purposes. This evidence might come through the written work, the maps and reports or through the adverts for fair-trade products that the class might produce. As ever, we would use a variety of approaches towards collecting and evaluating evidence of the pupil learning that arises from the Storyline activities.

Pupil ownership

So far we have considered curriculum planning from only one perspective. It is really important that the pupils are also consulted. They can be given some ownership of the learning and choice over what they want to find out. They can be given the feeling that it is they and not the teacher who holds the line. Many teachers will begin with a KWL grid, where pupils are asked, "What do you already know? What do you want to find out? What can we learn?" Key questions are devised by the pupils and the quest to find out is set. In Storyline this can still happen, yet it is in the interests of their 'family,' or in response to the 'challenge,' that they want to find out. As long as the teacher has researched the curricular possibilities and is able to develop an appropriate Storyline narrative, then the pupils can feel that they are in complete control of their learning, whilst the teacher will know that they are covering the required learning outcomes for this project.

Incidental learning

One aspect of any project on the rainforest is the artwork and classroom displays that go with it. There is so much scope to produce stunning work; on the forest itself, the wildlife and the sheer scale of the rainforest. I have not included this in the plan above, but you could provide a strong argument for having a focus on Literacy and Social Studies as well as Art and Design. The important thing is to have a clear focus on the planned learning, and to have clear strategies for gathering assessment evidence for the learning that takes place.

If you have the time and scope to develop a sequence of lessons to develop knowledge, skills and attitudes towards Art outcomes then this is a worthy aim. A good way to do this might be to have a parallel planner in place. The main interdisciplinary plan might include a focus on, for example, Social Studies and Literacy, but in tandem with that there might be another plan just for the Art development. This would mean that Art lessons could be planned that would provide a progressive learning opportunity for the pupils – and this would all be in the context of the rainforest. Skills and techniques could be taught and developed before being applied to the rainforest topic context.

Such an approach is quite different from 'doing a storyline' with lots of lovely art displays and claiming the class are 'learning about art.'

The distinction again would be: what is the planned learning in Art? How will you evidence the development of the skills for each pupil?

If you cannot answer these two fundamental questions, then you are not really 'teaching' them anything about art – you are merely providing them with opportunities to experiment or practice existing skills.

A detailed example of a storyline on the rainforest can be found in the Appendices.

Summary

In this chapter we have considered two different approaches towards using a storyline to deliver curriculum requirements. We have considered the approach where you might start with a great idea and then need to go to the curriculum to be able to justify using it in a storyline to develop the appropriate learning in your classroom. Then we considered an approach where we look at the curriculum first and use it to help us to identify exactly what kind of topic to plan. Either way, the next step is to involve the learners and to develop a meaningful context or story to motivate them to want to learn about this topic.

We looked at some examples of curriculum outcomes in terms of a project on the rainforest and stressed the need to maintain a focus on the planned learning outcomes. Incidental learning can be added to the plans at a later date. Finally, we considered the important role of assessment, and assessment evidence, and this is something we will look at in more detail in the next chapter.

11 Ways of presenting and assessing the learning

Planning, learning and assessment

In this book we have explored the huge learning potential of taking a Storyline approach. The interdisciplinary nature of Storyline means that it might be possible to develop learning on a number of fronts simultaneously. As stressed earlier in the book, it is important not to be fooled into thinking that it is possible to deliver deep learning in every curricular area you can think of to do with your narrative. If we want rich learning with some depth then we need to focus learning, and by implication assessment, on two or three curricular areas only.

Planned learning

In the examples we have looked at so far, the approach has been to plan for specific learning from these curricular areas and to think about assessment strategies and evidence to go with these plans. For example, in the previous chapter on planning a storyline we looked at the specific requirements of the curriculum and saw how activities could be designed to use a Storyline approach to deliver the experiences for the learners. It is not difficult then to find assessment evidence such as the notes taken by the teacher during the observation of talking activities or of pupil presentations. Nor would it be difficult to find written evidence of their understanding of knowledge, concepts or history connected with the storyline topic.

Looking back to the detailed plans in the previous chapter it is clear that we can plan learning that enables assessment to take place. We just need a systematic approach towards recording and evaluating the progress that takes place. We will look at this later on in this chapter.

The point is that we need to plan the learning and the assessment. If we can gather assessment evidence than we can be sure that the learning took place. If we cannot, then there is still work to do before we can say our learning intentions have been successful.

Incidental learning

In addition to the planned learning, there will always be some incidental learning that also takes place.

This might, for example, be connected to the planned learning but on a tangent that follows the pupils' interests - i.e. a rainforest storyline might provoke an interest in the design of traditional rainforest homes. Learning might follow which was not in the original plan but is significant learning nevertheless. Pupils might want to experiment with building their own models and testing strength, weatherproofing, etc. The process that follows may well deliver some rich experiences that would prove that learning had taken place under the Technology area of the curriculum. If this did happen then the teacher would be right to add this to their Storyline plan, retrospectively.

Assessment

In terms of assessment evidence it is useful to look at this in terms of:

1   things the learner can say;
2   things the learner can write;
3   things the learner can make;
4   things the learner can do.

Things the learner can say

Clearly the narrative approach provides a good deal of opportunity to develop skills in listening and talking. Teachers can find evidence of understanding simply by listening to the group discussions. As a group of children decide on the names, occupations and roles as a family in a WWII topic, for example, it will be clear if they have a notion that 'family' had a different composition then than it perhaps does today. The names and occupations too will give an insight into the learners' understanding of the era.

When the groups present their learning in a storyline using a challenge, such as *Dragon's Den*, it is easy for the teacher to draw up a checklist of the appropriate success criteria (ideally this should be compiled with input from the pupils) so that there is a common understanding of what it is that is being assessed. In this case it would be the design specification for the challenge, together with some of the skills of presenting to an audience.

Storyline affords opportunities to develop learning in the various types of talk: debates, presentations, collaborative group work and performance talk, to name just a few. For all of these there will be the content knowledge - provided by the authentic audience and purpose of the Storyline context, and the skills themselves associated with the various genres of talk listed above. Assessment should take account of the learning in both of these areas and the teacher should be able to create systems for doing this systematically. See the example below for one approach towards doing this.

102 *Assessment and planning approaches*

ASSESSMENT OF LEARNING: Date _____

Curricular area	
Learning intention	

	Success criteria				Assessment strategy
Needs more reinforcement	🔴				Formative Assessment used: • Thumbs up • Traffic lights • Two stars & wish • Peer comment • Peer marking • Self-marking • Show-me boards
Generally achieved/with support	🟡				
Achieved fully without support	🟢				

NAME	TRAFFIC LIGHTS			COMMENTS

So what have I learned about my teaching?		So what have I learned about specific pupil progress/needs with this learning?

IMPLICATIONS: So what, **specifically**, will I do about this next time?

-
-
-

Things the learner can write

There is a wide variety of writing that can be done in association with the Storyline approaches covered in this book. Almost every genre that is commonly taught in the primary school can be tackled through the authentic context of a narrative.

Below is a selection of genres taken from the curriculum in England and in Scotland, and for each of these genres some examples of writing that could easily be incorporated in a Storyline context.

Some of the storyline titles are featured in this book. Others might just inspire you to create your own topic based on the title, the writing idea and the input from your own class!

Genre of writing	Example	Storyline topic
Imaginative writing	Writing about what the owl gets up to during the night	The owl who was afraid
Diary entries	Diary entries from our alien visitor	Alien visitors
Scientific report	Testing materials and writing a report	A challenge from space
Persuasive letter	Trying to persuade a supermarket company not to build on our play park	Our street and the land developers
Directions	Explaining to our visitor how to get to our school	The visitor
Instructions	Explaining how our invention actually works	An enterprise challenge
Invitations	Invitations to our celebration, having saved the rainforest village	The rainforest
Poetry	Poems from the WWI trenches	WWI
Stories with historical settings	The Viking raiders come to our shores	Viking invaders
Recount	What happened on our trip	Standing stones
Newspaper article	Advertising for crew for our pirate ship	Pirates
Propaganda	'Dig for Victory' in WWII	WWII
Posters	Advertising our dream hotel by the sea	A dream hotel challenge
Advertising	Advertising our new household invention	An enterprise challenge
Instructions	Showing our alien visitor how to make toast/a sandwich	An alien visitor
Personal writing	How I felt when we went to visit the castle dungeons	Castles
Imagined personal	How I felt as the Romans attacked our village	The Roman Empire
Biography	Writing about our WWII families	WWII
Stories from different cultures	Making our own folk takes	The Great Wall of China
Information text	How to build an Anderson shelter	WWII

Things the learner can make

One of the attractions of the Storyline approach is that it can be so inclusive. It doesn't just rely on the traditional literacies of reading and writing. Pupils often shine when given the opportunity to share their learning through other activities such as painting, modelling and

104   Assessment and planning approaches

drama. Below are just a few ideas of things that they can make in order to demonstrate their understanding of knowledge or concepts, or with which they can show a set of skills that they have learned through a Storyline context.

Activity	Example	Storyline topic
Writing and book making	Making ration books and recipes	WWII
Model making	Models of a Viking longship	The Vikings
Model making	Model of Roman plumbing	The Romans
Design and make	Making our own inventions or products to sell	An enterprise challenge
Frieze/display	Making a display of our learning	Any topic
Video plan, film, edit	Making a documentary of our learning	Any topic
Technology	Making a solution to a given problem: making a means for the lighthouse keeper to get his lunch without the seagulls stealing it	The Lighthouse Keeper's Lunch
Art/craft	Making artefacts from the storyline to show what we know	Any topic
Mapping	Make a map, model or example and then explain to an audience what we know about this	Any topic

Things the learner can do

Below you will find some suggestions of things you can make and do that will demonstrate the learning in terms of knowledge, skill, concepts or general understanding. These ideas will provide assessment evidence for the teacher to record, analyse and inform next steps for planning future learning.

General ideas

The class can:

- hold celebrations, parties, outings;
- stage a drama to show what they know and what they imagine;
- present a quiz show involving what they have learned;
- demonstrate what they have learned – in terms of knowledge, skills and understanding;
- have an exhibition, open day or 'tour of artefacts.'

Other practical examples

Topic	Things to make/do	Things to do
The Middle Ages	A model castle (annotated) Research, plan and organise the food, costume, entertainment, etc., for a banquet	A mediaeval banquet
Vikings	A longship	Act out an invasion
The Romans	Models showing Roman plumbing	Demonstrate military strategies
Bridges	A variety of models	Create a documentary

The Lighthouse Keeper's Lunch: problem solving	A means for the lighthouse keeper to get his lunch without the seagulls stealing it	Conduct an interview with the 'expert' inventor
Alien visitor	A map of the solar system to help him get home	Make a stop-go animation of the solar system
The rainforest	A frieze showing the different layers and life of the rainforest	Debate whether or not to cut down more trees
Enterprise project	The products in response to design challenge	Pitch the benefits and efficacy of your product
Fairyland	A map and information about fairy customs, traditions and superstitions	A drama to show the problem and our solution
WWII	Ration books and recipes	What it was like to be evacuated
Life in the 1960s	A non-fiction text such as a map, timeline or fact file	Make a video
Dinosaurs	An exhibition	Become tour guides for our dinosaur (model) exhibition
The Highland Clearances	A performance to demonstrate understanding of what life was like during the Clearances	Drama/presentation

Visible learning

Nowadays it is not sufficient that the pupils learn. They also benefit from having some meta-cognition: understanding *how* we learn, as well as *what* we learn.

This was a topic covered in detail in my book *Metacognition in the Primary Classroom* (Routledge 2015), the idea being that pupils need to understand *how they learn*; their strengths, weaknesses and strategies for learning, so that they can be well equipped to make the most of their abilities.

This approach requires the teacher to involve the learner in decisions about their learning. They will model the 'language of learning' so that pupils are equipped to talk about how they learn and are able to evaluate their own progress, and can make decisions about ways to improve their approaches towards learning. These aims can be readily achieved through a Storyline approach. If teachers are involving the pupils in establishing success criteria and then affording them opportunities to talk about learning as they learn, then the learners will enjoy a much richer experience than ever before. The assessment of learning can then be jointly constructed by teacher and learner and, similarly, it can be assessed by them too.

For example, if the class are consulted right from the start about what they want to get out of their Storyline experience, they can also be involved in monitoring how they learn and what they learn. It may be that they want to celebrate their storyline on the Highland Clearances with an exhibition for parents. They may decide that they want to show them what they have learned about how the landscape of Scotland has changed, and the reasons why so many Scots ended up all over the globe. This criteria for success involves pupil participation, and ensures an authentic task with a genuine audience and purpose. The learners decide much of what is to be learned and how they will learn it, and most importantly they will have to consider the all-important assessment question: "After the learning has taken place, how will I know if I have actually learned it?"

Systematic assessment

Of course, every teacher has their own way of recording their assessment evidence. The important thing is that there is a systematic approach that enables you to monitor all children and not just the ones who stand out because they are doing so well or are finding it all too challenging.

One approach I have used for many years involves a list of pupils, a grid for the success criteria and a traffic light system for evaluating progress. I have used this for groups and for a whole class; I have used it to record observations of listening and talking and also for other curricular areas where the assessment evidence is more tangible. In the example I have shown how a newspaper article for our WWII topic might be recorded and assessed. The success criteria came from the pupils themselves, so we were all looking for the same thing.

ASSESSMENT OF LEARNING: Date _____

Curricular area	English Language: Functional writing (in the style of a newspaper) Persuasive writing
Learning intention	I am writing in the style of a newspaper article I can select and use vocabulary to persuade and inform

Success criteria					Assessment strategy
Needs more reinforcement 🔴 Generally achieved/with support 🟡 Achieved fully without support 🟢	I can write in columns using a headline and a subheading	I can use 'wow' words to persuade the reader	I can use facts from WWII to inform and persuade	I can adopt the style of a newspaper report	Formative Assessment used: • Thumbs up • Traffic lights • Two stars & wish • Peer comment • Peer marking • Self-marking • Show-me boards
NAME	**TRAFFIC LIGHTS**				**COMMENTS**
Cara	🔴	🟡	🟢	🟡	Some good facts used but forgot the subheading and needs to work on using more 'wow' words
Brodie	🟢	🟢	🟢	🟢	Some excellent work in the style of a newspaper. Needs now to try to use more journalistic words
Daniel	🟡	🟡	🟢	🟡	Some good links to journalistic conventions but needs to include more facts
Eva	🟢	🔴	🔴	🔴	Although it is set out like a newspaper there needs to be more detail (didn't finish this!)

Georgie	🟡	🟢	🟢	🟢	Forgot to write in columns until it was almost too late!
Hilda	🟢	🟢	🔴	🟡	A good attempt, but more detail needed, especially WWII-related information
So what have I learned about my teaching?				So what have I learned about specific pupil progress/needs with this learning?	
I need to check their understanding before I let them get started. Having a 'learning pit-stop' made a difference as it gave me a chance to remind some of them about writing in columns and using 'wow' words				Cara, Daniel, Eva and Georgie need support in processing the information. Next time I will get everyone to 'tell' their learning partner what they think they need to do for the task before they start working Eva needs a scaffolding sheet to help her to focus and structure her work and to provide more detail.	
IMPLICATIONS: So what, **specifically**, will I do about this next time?					
• Have strategies for them to check their understanding of the task set • Brainstorm facts to include with them and have this on the board • Have a 'learning pit-stop' to share success and put everyone back on track					

You will note that I have not stopped at recording pupil progress and evidence. I feel that there is no point in having a pretty grid recording what pupils did if you do not ask the 'so what?' question. As you can see, my 'so what?' considers what I learned about my lesson and the learning that did (or did not) take place. It also informs the 'Next time I will . . .' section, where I want to act upon the assessment in order to support and challenge pupils to do better next time.

Clearly this approach can be adapted to suit almost any learning that is planned. It allows for pupil engagement as they help to establish the success criteria, and it provides scope for pupils themselves to self-assess their own work or to assess the work of a peer.

You can find a blank version of this assessment format in the Appendices.

This is just one approach towards creating a manageable, meaningful and systematic assessment record. I have no doubt that experienced teachers who read this will have tried-and-tested approaches that are just as, if not more, effective!

Summary

Classrooms are busy places and there are lots of demands on teacher time – both in and out of class. Therefore, if we can design some of the learning where we can target the teaching, recording and assessing of learning for different areas of the curriculum simultaneously, we will be able to maximise the impact of our time. Clearly the interdisciplinary approach enables us to do this. It is important to provide opportunities for pupils to demonstrate the depth of their understanding by applying skills and knowledge in unfamiliar contexts. A storyline provides these contexts so that, for example, skills in maths, language or technology might be employed in order to solve a problem.

Assessment and planning approaches

In this chapter we have looked at ways of having a focus on just one or two curricular areas and to consider what and how to assess the learning. We have considered the fact that there will inevitably be some incidental learning that takes place and this can be recorded after the event. We also looked at different ways of conducting assessment and recording this for evaluation to take place in order to arrive at next steps in planning the learning.

Once you have a clear idea of what you want them to learn and an understanding of how you will assess it and provide evidence of this learning, you will be free to use a Storyline approach secure in the knowledge that the required learning objectives can be achieved whilst the class can have all the fun of learning with passion!

Part IV

Appendices – practitioner examples, plans, case studies and templates

1   Storyline in a day
2   Alien writing frame
3   Practitioner example: Alien Story
4   Practitioner example: WWII plan
5   Practitioner example: Highland Clearances (the Street)
6   Practitioner example: Wizard School (the Street)
7   Practitioner example: Mary Queen of Scots
8   Practitioner example: Forest School (the Letter)
9   Practitioner example: Our Railway
10 Practitioner example: The Middle Ages (the Challenge)
11 Practitioner example: Egypt
12 Practitioner example: Wind Farm
13 Practitioner example: New Neighbours and Refugees (the Street)
14 Synopsis planning pro forma
15 Storyline planning pro forma
16 Storyline planning template
17 WWII complete synopsis
18 WWII complete plan
19 Rainforest complete synopsis
20 Rainforest complete plan
21 Deforestation example
22 Assessment pro forma
23 Completed assessment grid
24 Using templates

Appendix 1

Storyline in a day

Aliens

Learning: Literacy and Expressive Arts

| Imaginative personal writing | Oral storytelling | Art |
| Persuasive writing | Drama | Listening and talking |

Process: eight groups of four

Teacher: We are going to think about aliens from another planet. What might they look and sound like? What might they be called? What interests and hobbies might they have? In your group discuss ideas you might have. [Listening and talking]

112 *Appendices*

1 You are going to become an alien family from another planet so decide who is who and where you are from. [Listening and talking]

Appendix 1 113

2. Using the materials provided and the techniques modelled, you will now create a family portrait. Each person will be represented. Please annotate the portrait to show each person's name age and interests. [Art]

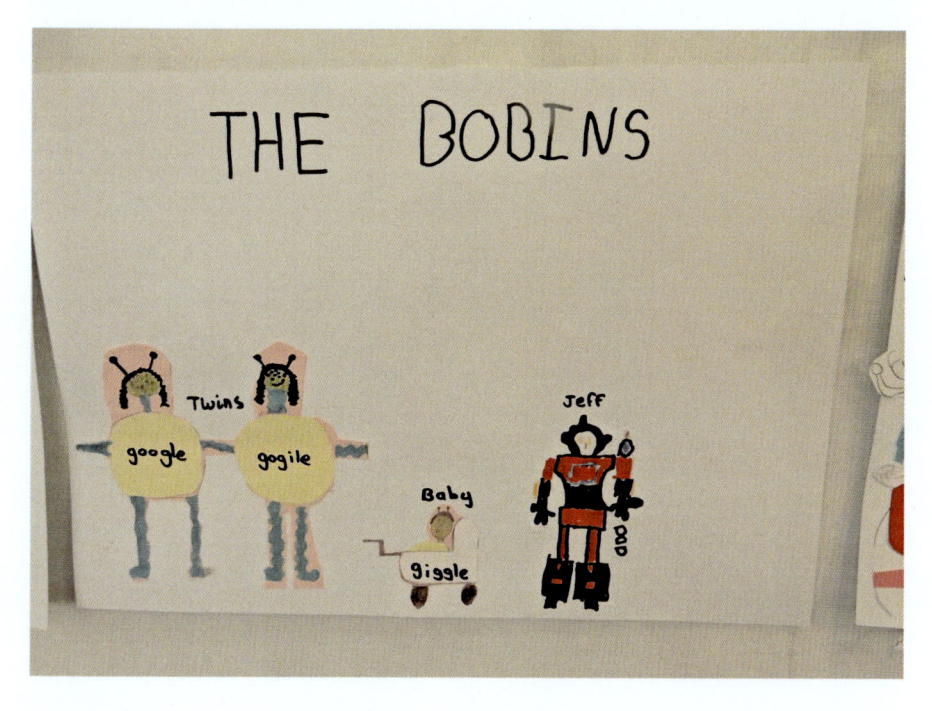

114 *Appendices*

3   Each family needs a home. Using the materials provided and the techniques modelled you will now create a home for your family. Again, you might need to annotate the home in order to show any interesting or unusual features. [Art]

4   We want to know something about you. Write a brief introduction about yourself. Tell us things like: what is your name? Where are you from? How old are you? Who is in your family and what do you do all day? What special talent do you have? [See Appendix 2: Alien Writing Frame.] You can do this task on your own or in pairs. [Imagined personal writing]
5   Imagine what life might be like on your home planet. What will everyone do? What will they eat and drink? How will they entertain themselves? Share your ideas on what life is like for your family.
6   You will now go to meet another family. You will tell them all about yourself, your family and your home. In pairs you will first tell the others and then listen to them. [Oral storytelling]
7   Bad news! An asteroid shower is heading your way and your planet will be destroyed. The only option is to leave your planet. The nearest planet that would support your life is called the Earth. You must send them a message: you need help. You need them to agree to take you in as refugees. How will you persuade them to take you in? In your group prepare your message – it can take the form of a poster, letter, email or a series of annotated pictures – but hurry, you need to complete the message in 20 minutes before all communications cease! [Persuasive writing]

Envelopes

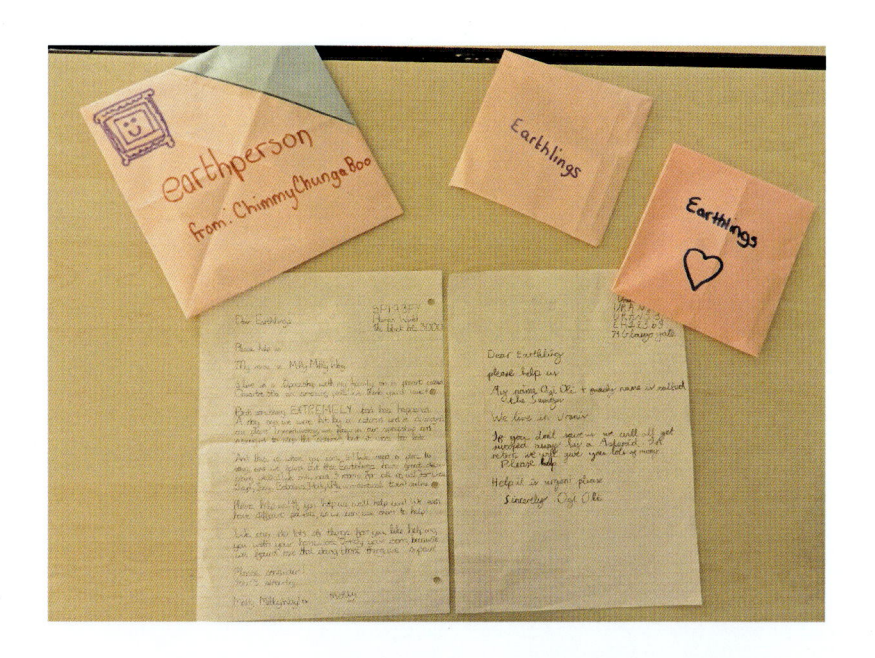

- **earthperson** from: ChimmyChungaBoo
- Earthlings
- Earthlings ♥

Letter 1 (Molly)

Dear Earthlings

Please help us

My name is Molly MilkyWay

I live in a spaceship with my family on a planet called [...] think you'd love.

But something EXTREMELY bad has happened. A big asteroid was hit by a natural [...] and it destroyed our planet transmissions. We flew in our spaceship and managed to escape the asteroid, but it was too late [...]

And this is where you come in! We need a place to stay, and we found that Earthlings have great decorating skills! We only need 3 rooms for all of us! For Uncle Jagd, Joey, Bobolus, Holly (My un-identical twin) and me.

Please help us! If you help us, we'll help you! We each have different powers, so we can use them to help!

We can do lots of things for you, like helping you with your homework & tidy your room, because we found out that doing those things are a pain!

Please consider!
Your's sincerely,

Molly MilkyWay!xx   Molly

Letter 2 (Ogi Olli)

Dear Earthling

Please help us

My name is Ogi Olli & mum's name is called Sista Sawyer

We live in Venus

If you don't save us we will all get sucked away by a Asteroid that means we won't give you lots of money.
Please help.

Help is urgent please

Sincerely Ogi Olli

8 In the next episode you journey to the Earth. On the way you have an adventure. In your group think about how you might show an audience how you hear the news about the asteroid, pack up and leave. What adventure do you have? How do you finally land on the Earth? [Drama]
9 Join with another group. One family will be the aliens and the other will be Earthlings. Using 'still pictures' show what happens when they meet. Now bring the pictures to life. [Drama]
10 You need to find a new planet for the alien family. Earth cannot meet all of their needs. Research the solar system and find them somewhere to stay. Create a poster, leaflet or information text that will convince then that this is the best place for their new home. [Persuasive writing]
11 Think about how we can end our storyline day. How can we show that all the aliens got to their new homes safely? How can we celebrate our learning as a class? Now that we have got our friends home safely it is time to think about learning:

    a   Make a list of the curriculum subjects you think our topic has covered.
    b   Can you recall three or more facts about planets or space?
    c   List at least five learning skills or dispositions you used during this project.
    d   Write at least two sentences about something that you enjoyed.
    e   Write at least two sentences about something that you might have liked to do more of or to have done differently.

Appendix 2

Alien writing frame

My alien

First, tell us your own name and family name:

Describe yourself:

Where do you live?

118 *Appendices*

What do you do during the day? Do you have a job or hobby?

What special talent do you have?

What else can you say about yourself?

Draw an illustration of you doing what you like to do best:

Appendix 3

Practitioner example: Alien Story

By Daryl Gladstone (who was a student on placement at the time)

Phase 1: the event

The alien appeared in class after a lunch break. For effect, the window was open and classroom items had been knocked over where the alien's rocket had landed. The children arrived and began to investigate the scene – they found the alien along with a letter from him.

The letter told the class the name of the alien and his home planet; his name was Gus. Gus wanted their help; he wanted to learn about the Earth. This prompted a lot of discussion and together the class created a mind map based on what the children thought Gus should learn.

This provided an opportunity for the teacher to gently guide their responses, with the intention that we would be using a Storyline approach to explore the space project. As this Storyline example began near to Christmas that also became a suggestion.

After the mind map was created I then thought about the direction the storyline would go. However, I wanted it to be mostly child-led, so I intended for it to remain flexible. Without making dreaded 'tenuous links' I aimed to focus on only a few curricular areas, all based on what the children had suggested: Art, Science, Maths, Health and Wellbeing and RME.

Phase 2: Art, Science and Maths

To commence our space learning our classroom was converted into a spaceship, encouraging lots of role-play. The children also created their own intergalactic passports to begin their learning journey. We focused our learning on the Sun, Moon and stars – along with learning about the time during Mathematics. The children also wanted to know about the planets, so our learning changed direction slightly as we touched upon the different planets in our solar system. Focusing on naming the planets, the activities included planet collages as well as papier mâché planets made with our learning partners.

Phase 3: Health and Wellbeing, RME and (unexpectedly!) Technology

During this phase of the storyline the children received another letter from Gus. He was enjoying his time with them but sometimes felt very lonely when they were not there. Once again, the children brainstormed what they could do to help. They wanted to make him some alien friends, and so they did. Christmas was drawing nearer so the children taught Gus why we celebrate Christmas. They knew that Gus was going home to celebrate Christmas on his own planet. Then our storyline took an unexpected turn: one day a child dropped Gus' rocket in front of the class, and part of it broke off. They suddenly feared that Gus would not be able to travel back home. However, this now opened a new storyline door, and we decided that we could make a new rocket for Gus. So, using recyclable materials the children worked in pairs to build new rockets. We focused our learning on the different features of a rocket and what they should all have, planning our design before assembling it.

However, upon choosing the best rocket that fitted Gus' criteria the children then realised that their leftover rockets were redundant. That was until one child chipped in with a perfect suggestion, which for me tied together the learning undertaken during the storyline: "Now Gus' alien friends can fly home with him."

This was a fantastic idea and everyone was happy with the suggestion. All of the aliens the class had created could now have a rocket to travel back to Gus' home planet. Our Christmas party doubled up as a leaving party as we waved goodbye to our new friend Gus.

Assessment

During this topic, different methods of assessment were used to track learning. I documented the progress of our storyline using a floor book, tracking all of our learning and sharing it with the class. I had also set up a blog at the start of the school year to share learning with parents; it contains pictures and videos of the children taking part in and discussing their learning. So at different stages of our storyline I would stop and film children talking about what they had been learning in class – this gave a great overall insight into their perspective.

This learning was fun, active and child-led and, more importantly to the children, it was real. The children empathised with Gus, they cared about him and they were motivated by the idea of them learning along with him.

Appendix 4

Practitioner example: WWII plan

Lesson 1: KWL grid

Pupils completed KWL grids and discussed what they already knew about WWII, what they would like to find out, how they would learn it and how they would be assessed.

Lesson 2: introduction and families

I played Neville Chamberlain's 'declaration of war speech' without any introduction or link to our storyline. We then discussed what the clip meant and how people would be feeling at that time.

I then explained that we were going to be learning about WWII through a storyline, and to do that we needed each to have a character and to be part of a family. The class split into groups of three to discuss their family set-up (would their family have a dad, grandmother, children, etc.?), and then began making their character with available resources. We used lollipop sticks as a base with Blu Tack on the bottom, so the characters could be moved around easily.

Lesson 3: 1940s house

Using 1940s footage about the kitchen, living room, dining room, bedroom and bathroom from the Imperial War Museum website (www.iwm.org.uk/collections/item/object/1060023055), the children compared and contrasted their home to a 1940s home. The notes taken from the videos informed their family trios' plans for their own homes.

Lessons 4 and 5: making houses

Using their previous plans, the children created their family's WWII home using the resources available.

We created a list of shared success criteria with things the house should contain; for example, blackout blinds and a radio/wireless.

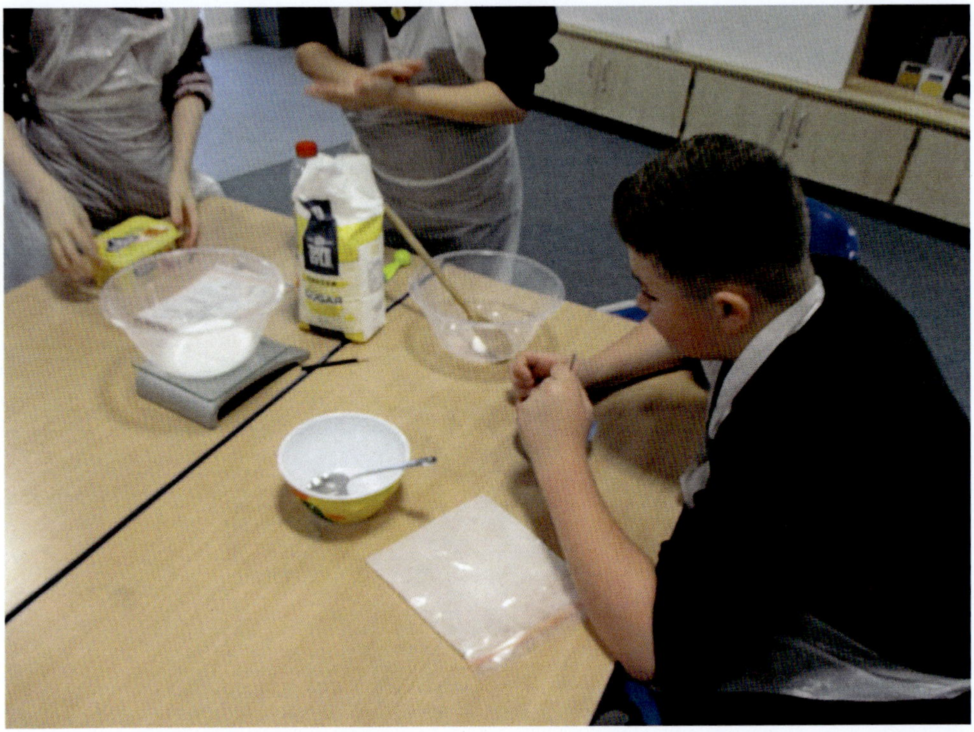
SUGAR

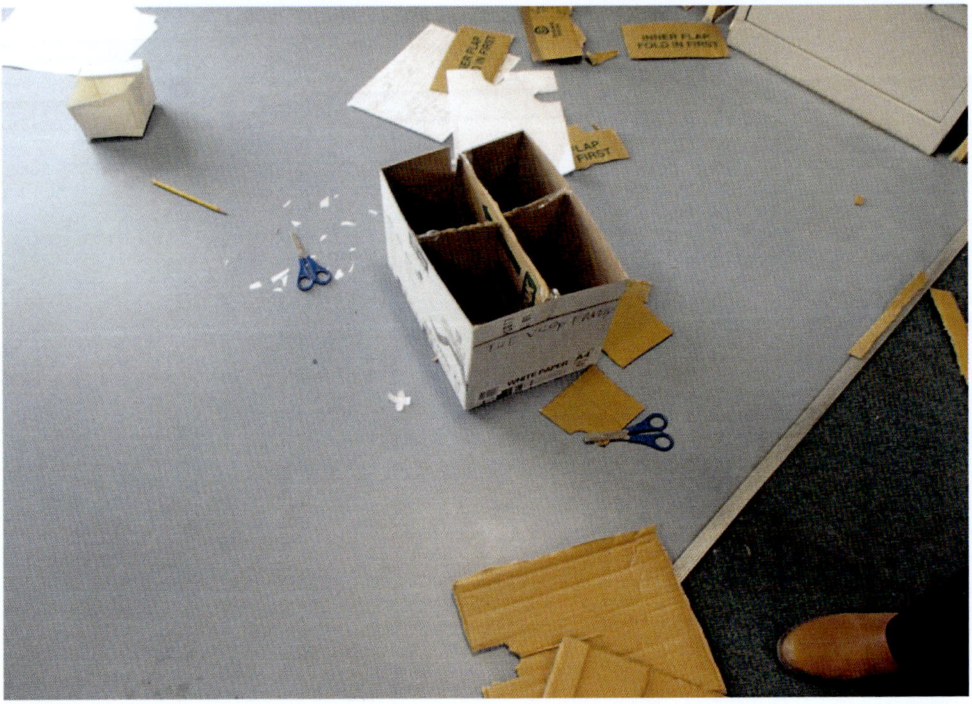
INNER FLAP
FOLD IN FIRST

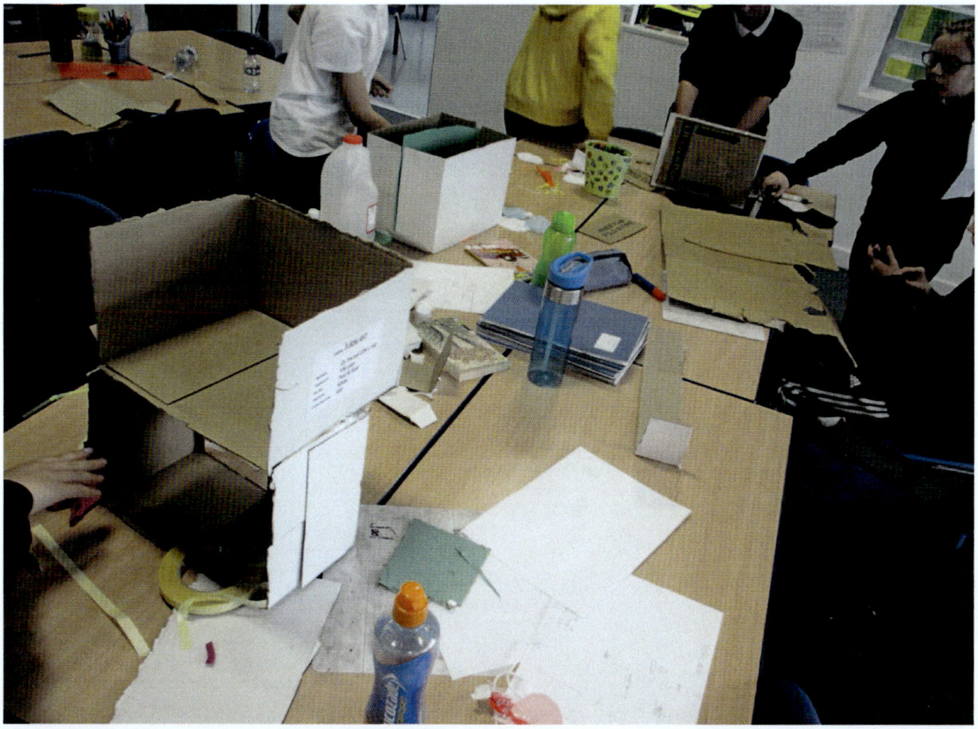

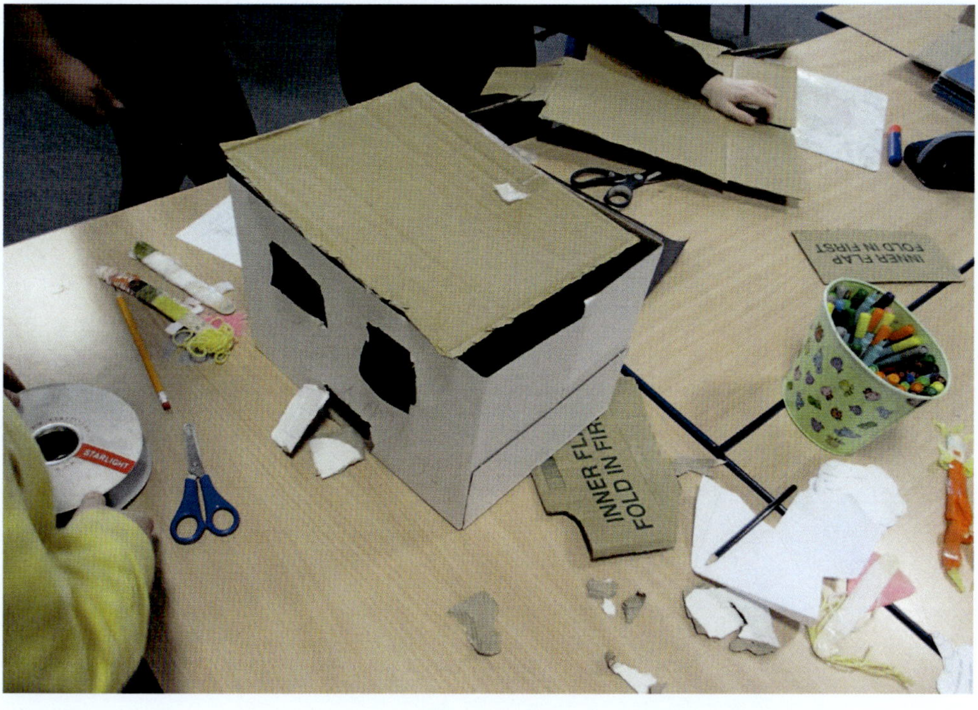
INNER FLAP
FOLD IN FIRST
INNER FL
FOLD IN FIR
STARLIGHT

Lesson 6: rationing

The class watched the clip 'Food Flash – The ration books are coming' (www.iwm.org.uk/search/global?query=FOOD+FLASH&pageSize=) to introduce rationing.

We had a whole-class discussion on what rationing was and why it was needed during WWII.

After this discussion, I asked one member of each family to check their house to see if anything had changed. I had put an envelope in each house containing a leaflet on dried eggs with different recipes taken from a WWII recipe book, and a small bag of dried eggs. We discussed the sponge/cupcake recipe they would be making, and put the learning into context by making it the birthday of someone in their family. The groups then worked collaboratively to bake their cakes, and enjoyed tasting them and comparing them to 'normal' cakes!

Lesson 7: air raids and Anderson shelters

After lunch, the class came in to an air raid noise in the background. We discussed what this noise meant and what air raids and Anderson shelters were, with a PowerPoint to aid the discussion. We then pushed all the tables into the centre of the classroom and moved the chairs to the side to allow the children to explore how people would have felt during this through drama in their family trios. We had discussed the procedure for when the air raid siren was sounded, so as part of the drama I asked the groups to imagine they were getting ready for bed. During this, I played the air raid siren and the pupils dived under our class 'Anderson shelter.' We also had an air raid siren from WWII, so we tried this out too.

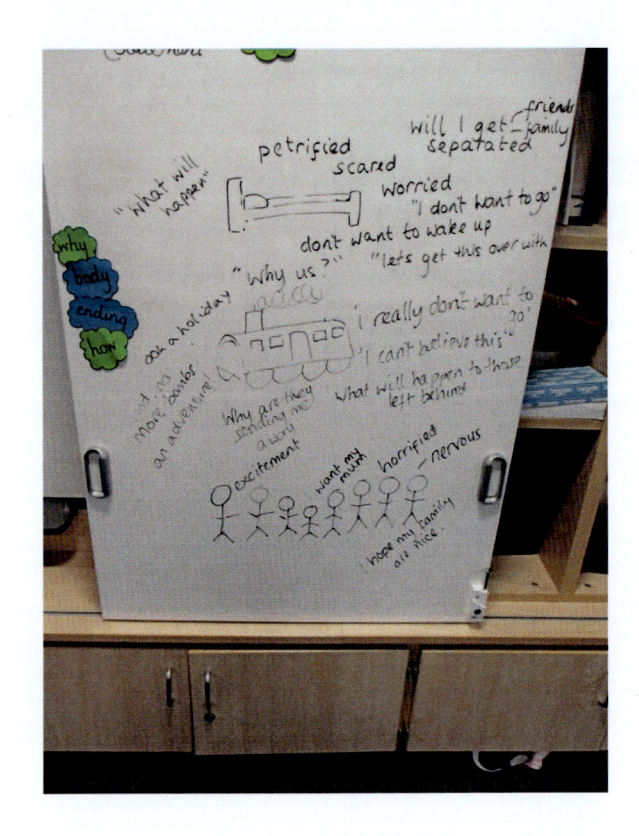

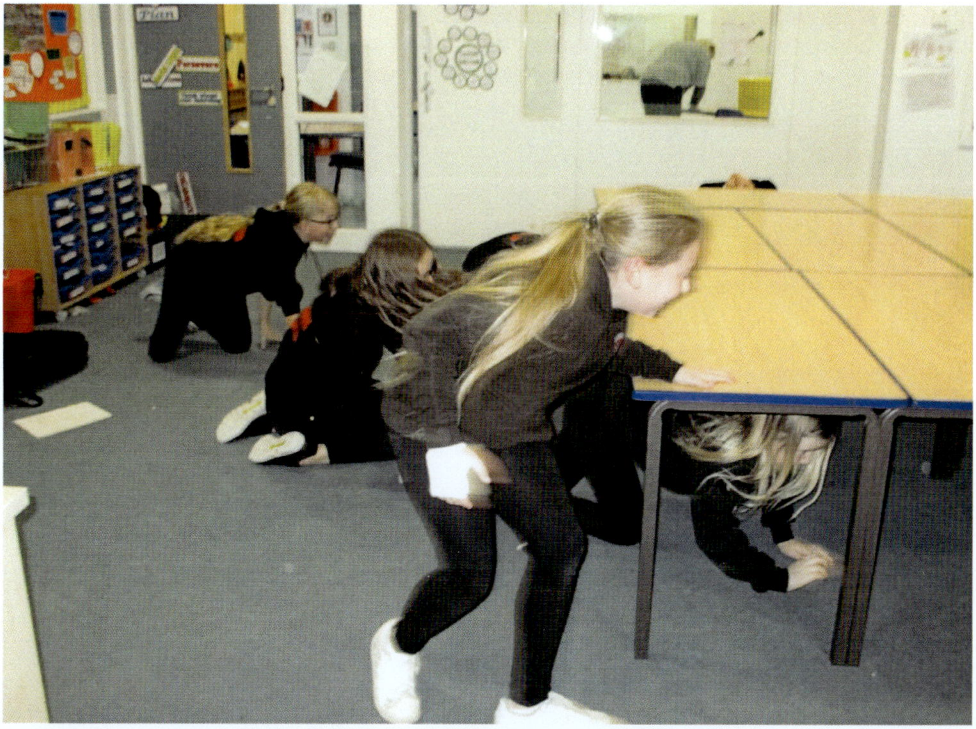

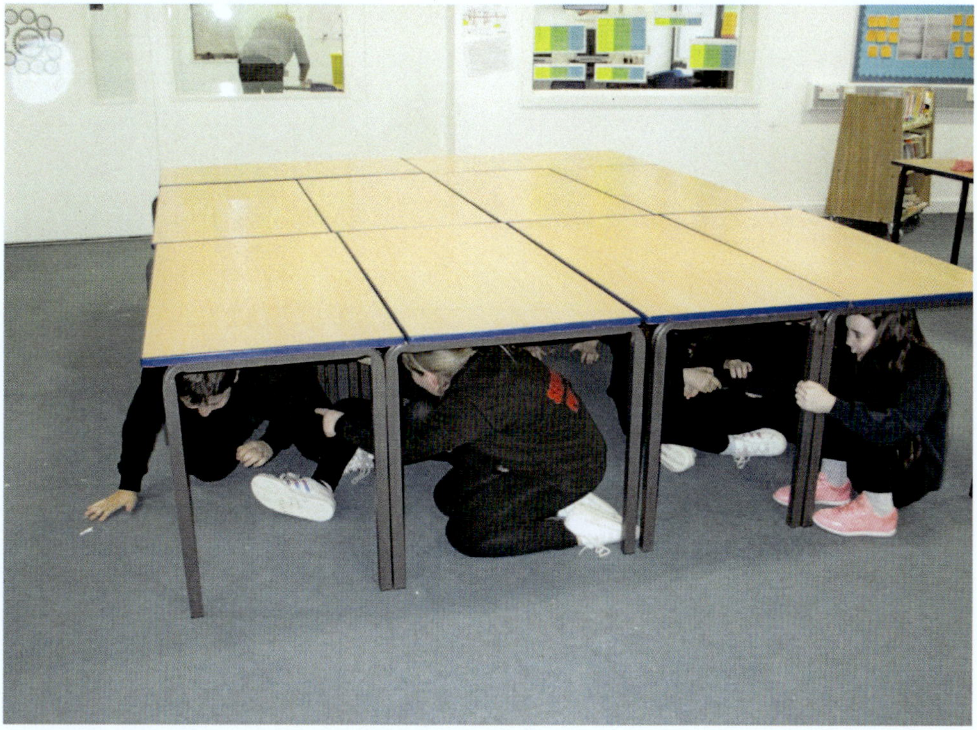

126 *Appendices*

Lesson 8: the Blitz

I used the Primary History WWII website (www.bbc.co.uk/schools/primaryhistory/world_war2/) for the initial discussion with the class about the Blitz. We then looked at some short-story examples of people's own accounts and experiences of life during the Blitz. After discussion, the class split into their family trios to plan their characters' diary entry of their experience during the Blitz, and then wrote this on lined paper which we later tea-stained to make it look old and worn.

Lessons 9 and 10: evacuation

To introduce Evacuation, we watched the clip 'Evacuation: Episode 1' (www.bbc.co.uk/programmes/b0079c8p). This explained what evacuation was and the process of it, and what the children were required to do and take, including gas masks. We then prepared for our own evacuation by making identity tags and gas-mask boxes to carry on our journey.

On the day of the 'evacuation,' children were asked to bring a small suitcase/rucksack packed with a change of clothes, a small toy and a book. The children thoroughly enjoyed bringing these and sharing with the class what they had brought. We invited parents to walk with us to the nearby train station and wave us off as we boarded the train. We sorted children into families to make the experience as real as possible. After we got off the train at the next stop we walked back to class.

Lesson 11: VE Day

To conclude our WWII topic, we ended with a VE Day celebration party. We discussed what VE Day meant and how this would have affected the lives of people during WWII. We played table games at the party and tried some Spam sandwiches too!

Appendix 5

Practitioner example: Highland Clearances (the Street)

By Annie Stockdale (who was a student on her final placement at the time)

Lesson 1: building the clan

We discussed what a typical clan might look like in terms of family members and what they would wear. We also discussed how each clan would have had their own tartan.

The classes were split into four different groups. Each group made their own 'clan.' After that they named and 'built' their own croft house and added some animals (mainly sheep).

Following this, each clan discussed their relationships with the other clans, and how they felt about living in the area which they named 'Fort X.' We discussed how the clans had to pay rent to a tacksman, who forwarded this money to the Laird of Fort X, and how they felt about this. This lesson gave pupils a rich opportunity for learning about Highland townships and clan life. I asked the children to keep a close eye on the board throughout the week.

128 *Appendices*

In the days that followed, I added more sheep to the board. This was to represent the laird wanting to keep more sheep on the land. I also put signs on the board that read 'Final rent request.'

The day before the second lesson I made a 'tacksman' with a warning and put him on the board.

Lesson 2: a visit from the laird

This lesson was aimed to teach the children about the laird's decisions concerning the Highland townships, and what this meant for the clans.

When the children came into the classroom, a 'laird' had appeared on the board with letters to the clans as well as to his tacksman. The letter to the clans explained that the laird wanted to keep more sheep on the land, and so the clans would have to leave. The letter also told the clans that they had not been paying their rent, and a forced eviction would follow if they did not leave promptly. The letter written to the tacksman from the laird explained to the tacksman that he would have to evict the clans from Fort X, and told him how things would change following the clan's departure.

The pupils were up in arms! By this stage, they had an emotional connection to their clans, and felt that it was unjust as the clans "had been working the land for many years." Each pupil had a photograph of their clan in their jotters with blank speech bubbles for each of the family members. They worked individually to complete these speech bubbles, which were very expressive indeed!

To assess this lesson, we had a hot-seating session in which we had the 'laird' in the hot seat. The clanspeople questioned the laird and explained why they were upset and why they didn't want to leave Fort X. The pupils were challenged to think about the different points of view and what they thought would be a good solution.

Before the following lesson, I put another speech bubble next to the tacksman which said, "You have been warned enough times. The laird is not going to be happy."

Lesson 3: forced evictions

In the morning before school started I put flames on the crofts to represent the houses being on fire. I also put on 'fire sounds' through the sound system in the classroom.

When the children came into the classroom and saw their houses on fire, they were in uproar.

I only wish I had filmed their reactions. I removed most of the people off the board as I thought this would cause less distress.

We looked at various learning materials about the more forceful evictions and wrote letters to other family members about what was happening in Fort X.

The children learnt about what happened to the clans during these forced evictions and what they would have experienced.

Lesson 4: emigration

This naturally led on to a lesson about emigration, and teaching the children about what emigration was and what the clans experienced during and after it. I led a discussion on what happened to the clans following this eviction. One of the pupils said, "Why don't we change our board into the sea and put our clans in boats heading to wherever they were sent to?"

I was only too happy for this to take place! As a class, we looked at emigration and watched media clips about the experiences of some families on the boats, where they ended up and what jobs they did. We then made boats and popped the clans in. The pupils wrote postcards from their clan to another clan that they liked, to explain where they were going and what they were going to do when they got there.

To assess the topic as a whole, each clan made a Puppet Pals presentation on their iPads, which told the story of their clan during the Clearances.

These presentations showed that the children really had grasped the concepts about the Clearances and what this meant for the people who lived in the Highlands.

The pupils and I really enjoyed this approach to teaching. The class teacher was very pleased with how the children had done, and said that she was looking forward to trying out this approach in other learning contexts!

12-2-15

Highland Clearances – The reactions of the clans

"I am very sad! Baby Taycon is only one hour old. I think the Laird is stupid"

"I command you to kill the Laird and the tax man"

Laird

tacksman

"I am mad. I am going to kill him and his stupid tax man. And rip their heads off And shoot him with a bow and arrow"

"I am going to ride on my demon sheep and kill him."

Brilliant Matthew. Good use of punctuation too.

Appendix 6

Practitioner example: Wizard School (the Street)

By Stephanie Waugh (who was a student teacher at the time)

Some of the children in my Upper Years primary school class had shown some interest in the Harry Potter books and all things Hogwarts.

This prompted me to try to harness this interest and enthusiasm to advance their learning, so I developed the storyline outlined below.

Lesson 1: who?

1   I told the class that we were going to create a wizard family.
2   I then gave out wizard templates to each table.
3   Each individual picked a template and created a character and gave them a name.
4   Each group had then to choose a family name and crest.

Lesson 2: who?

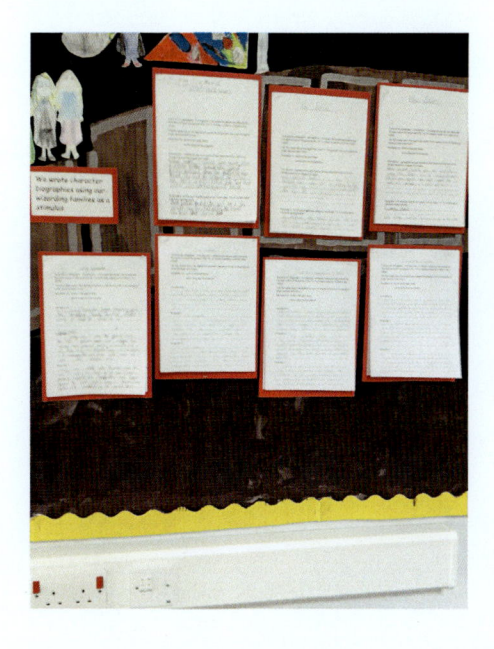

134 *Appendices*

1 We did some work on writing character descriptions and biographies and then shared these with the rest of the class.

Lesson 3: where?

1 We discussed where a wizard might live and agreed that we were all going to live in the same street.
2 We discussed what the homes might look like but then introduced a famous artist, Hundertwasser, and looked at some of his work.
3 We then looked at some of the houses from *Harry Potter*.
4 Each group was given materials to create their own home. Each family member had to do their own part of the house before assembling them all into a family home for the frieze.
5 Each group then 'introduced' their home and told everyone something about it.

Lesson 4: where?

I asked the children:

1. Think about daily life in your town and home.
2. Discuss as a group and class the sort of town you live in and what you think daily like might be like with your family (brainstorm).
3. Who are your friends?
4. What would it be like if new people moved in?
5. How would you act?

Lesson 5: what?

1. The class were asked to come up with an incident: "What might happen in your street? Something big – a car crash – or something small: a lost bin? Discuss and share with the class." (This was a short talking lesson just before break.)
2. After break, the children came in to see that on our display the 'Forbidden Forest' had a 'For sale' sign on it. There was a definite reaction! We discussed in groups who might buy it and what they might do with the land. They decided that they did not want it to be changed, so they decided to protest. They had a choice of writing a persuasive letter or a news article campaigning against the sale, or creating a detailed poster in protest.

Lesson 6: what?

1. I wrote them letters to say that their protest had been successful and the forest was saved! Instead, I put up a block of flats right next to their homes in the street.
2. They discussed who might move in and how those people might react to a street of neighbours who were all wizards!
3. I created a family and told the children about them whilst they took notes and then did character descriptions/illustrations based on this information.
4. We discussed how their characters might interact (or not) with each of the new residents.

Lesson 7: what?

1. Each group then had to make up a story of an incident that occurred between them and the new family. We did this as drama and used conventions like 'role on the wall' and 'conscience alley' to show how the characters were feeling.
2. Each story had to have a satisfactory ending, and later they wrote their own version of the story from the perspective of their character

Lesson 8: celebration

1. We discussed how we might end the story, and they opted for a wizard party. Each family had to do some sort of magic trick and to bring in some wizard-themed food or drink.
2. A great time was had by all!

Lesson 9: plenary

1 Finally, we reviewed the whole project and talked about all of the skills and knowledge we had developed in literacy, drama and art.

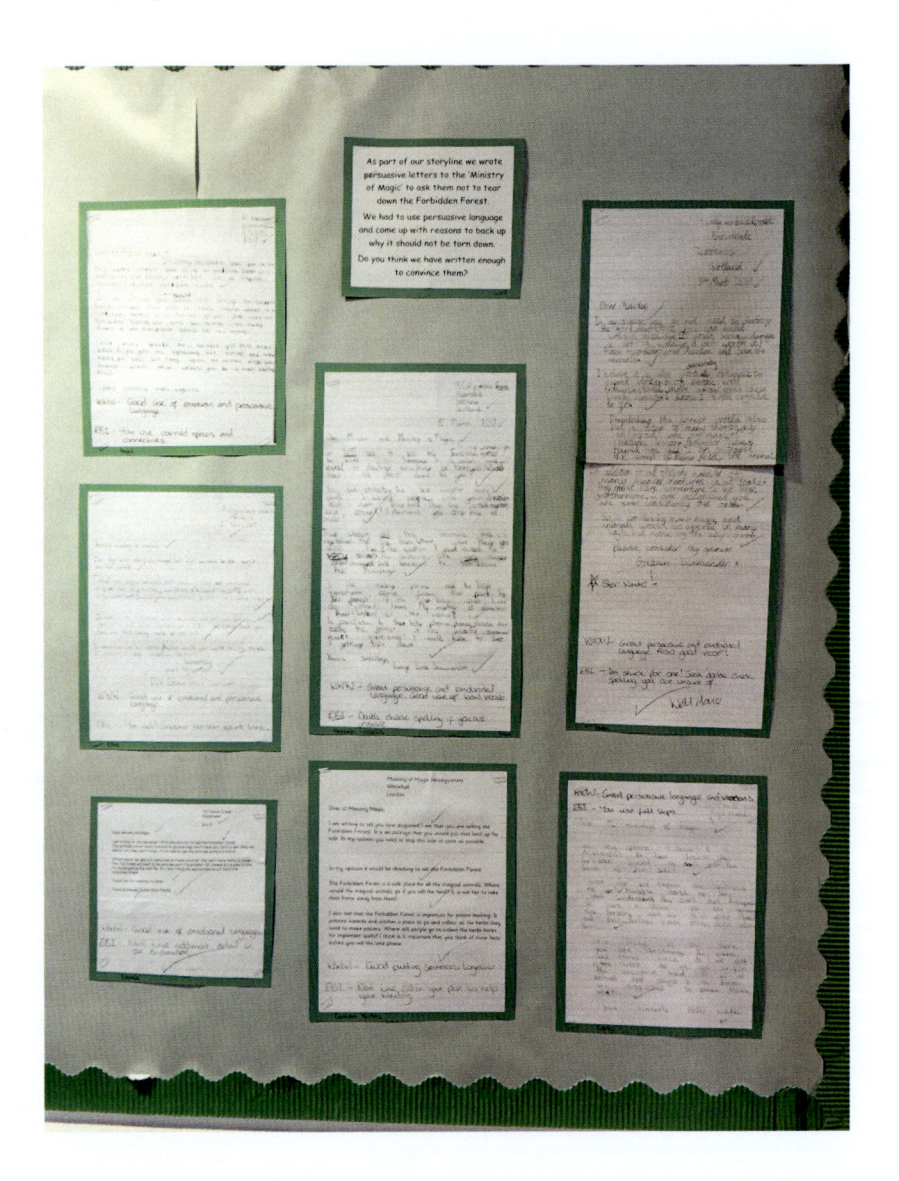

Appendix 7

Practitioner example: Mary Queen of Scots

A storyline using the conventions of the Visitor and the Letter

By Belinda Cook (who was a student teacher at the time)

138   *Appendices*

I did a storyline in my Middle Years placement on Mary Queen of Scots and the death of Lord Darnley.

It had been triggered by a pupil telling me what they had learned about Mary and saying that she had killed her second husband. I was aware that this wasn't proven and used this to do some critical-thinking interdisciplinary work that brought together non-fiction, reading comprehension, creative/factual writing and Social Studies/History.

I started out with a 'herald' (my class teacher dressed up) delivering letters to the children from prominent people of the time, asking them to set up newspapers and giving them all press passes.

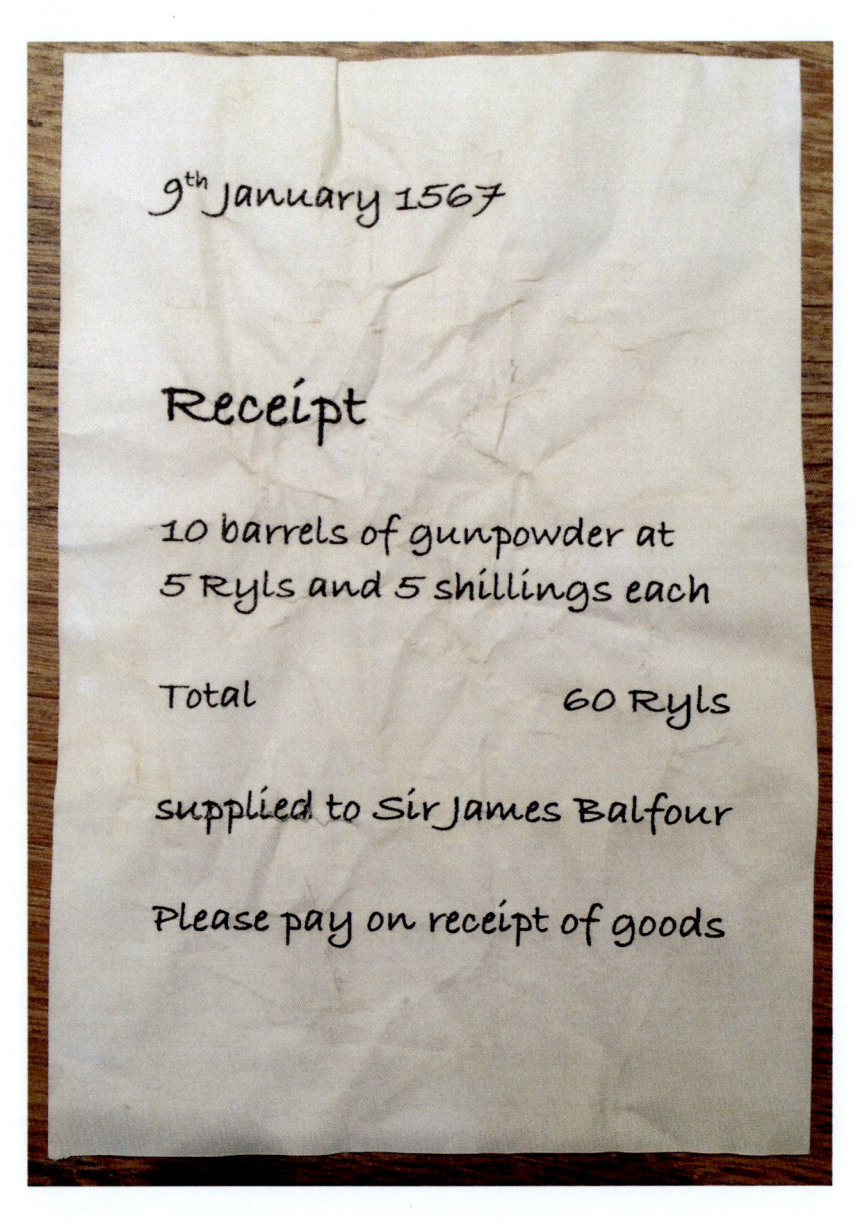

9th January 1567

Receipt

10 barrels of gunpowder at 5 Ryls and 5 shillings each

Total   60 Ryls

supplied to Sir James Balfour

Please pay on receipt of goods

The children, in groups, had to research what they might call their paper and design a header, then research a price for their paper and start to create appropriate adverts for it.

They came in after lunch one day to see that the wall had suffered from an explosion. There was also the outline of a body on the floor.

After their reaction and questions had subsided they were given envelopes containing evidence.

There was a town guard's report of the explosion, a receipt for gunpowder, a burnt letter fragment, a narrative from that time and a letter from Lord Darnley to Mary.

They then received a mocked-up gossip mag front page stirring up trouble for Mary. I had hoped that they would be critical of this, but they were all ready to string up Mary after this!

I then added an extra front page to stir things up further and get them to see the different stories that were circulating.

Finally, I got some P7s to dress up as Mary, the Earl of Bothwell and the Earl of Moray, and the class interviewed them to get their final bits of evidence.

The groups then worked out what they were going to report and what their version of events was, and split into writers and illustrators to do this. I was really pleased with the diversity of the stories they came up with, from Darnley and his manservant accidentally strangling themselves on the rope as they escaped to various individual groups carrying out the murder.

I had not originally planned to do a storyline on my first proper placement but I was really excited to do this when the idea was prompted by my conversation with a pupil. I think that there was some really good learning in it, though I do think there would be a lot of work on critical thinking to be done still as only two pupils *really* questioned the evidence put before them. I also had a great time doing all the prep for it and it was so much fun to teach this way.

> Finally I send you my kindest wishes and want to let you know that both you, my dearest Earl of Bothwell, and James Douglas the 4th Earl of Morton, have my full support and loyalty and I assure you that I no longer consider myself a protégé of Darnley.
>
> Yours faithfully
> James Balfour

Appendix 8

Practitioner example: Forest School (the Letter)

By Linda Murray, St Peter's Primary School, Galashiels, Scottish Borders

Forest School is an outdoor-based learning strategy which offers children the opportunity to investigate and explore their surroundings, manage their own risk and learn new skills without the constriction of a classroom. It is both child-led and child-initiated. When I take children up into the woods for their first experience, I like to use the Storyline approach to ease them into the process. Invariably, I am working with classes not my own and Storyline gives me the opportunity to learn more about the children, their needs and interests, very quickly. Usually, a Forest School block in our school is run over six weeks, but this block was scheduled close to the end of the school year and consequently ran for four weeks.

Week 1

Initially, I am generally looking to give the children opportunities to explore their site; to feel comfortable in their surroundings and to consider how they can manage their own risk. These areas of learning can be challenging for some children, particularly those who have little or no experience of woodlands or having freedom to explore without their hands being held (quite literally) throughout. Some worry terribly about getting messy.

Before the first session, the children had been introduced to a new storybook. As we all know, there are dozens to choose from, but one I find consistently successful, and requested by colleagues, is *Bare Bear*, written by Miriam Moss with illustrations from Mary McQuillan and published by Hodder Children's Books in 2005.

Busby is a little bear who wakes up one morning to find his clothes have been blown away in a storm. He heads off to search for them and makes various friends along the way who help him to find his clothes. It is written in rhyme and instantly appeals to children. Last May, in collaboration with the Primary 1 teacher Mrs Johnston, we held a very successful Forest School block based around this tale.

As we left for Forest School for the first session, a letter was delivered to us by our office administrator with instructions to read it when we were settled on our site. You can imagine the speculation and discussion this generated, not to mention the added incentive to climb the hill to our woodland, which for many was a completely new experience. The letter was deliberately hand-written rather than typed and was in messy script. On the way up the hill, Mrs Johnston and I made occasional references to a possible sense of someone watching us, but conveyed no

Appendix 15

Storyline planning pro forma

Way in/introduction/hook

Elements	*Questions*	*Learning*	*CfE Outcomes & Experiences*	*Activities*	*Evidence/ assessment*
Place Time Characters					
Normal daily life					
Unusual event					
Turning point or decision					
Resolution/ celebration					

This storyline could take about 10 sessions. This could mean two to three weeks' worth of Social Studies and Literacy lessons on the timetable

Appendix 8 141

feelings of anxiety or worry. Once settled, with boundaries and rules covered, the children sat for a snack and the letter was finally released from its envelope. As soon as the opening couple of sentences were read, children realised that the letter must be from Busby. Great excitement!

In the letter, Busby asked the children to find his clothes for him, as he was sure they were scattered around the woods. The children set off with gusto, and before long all the clothes were found. In the meantime, children were learning about their environment, beginning to understand that they needed to watch where they were going – for example, deep leaves may mean a dip in the land, or a slope may be slippery and will need more care – or even spot spaces they wanted to explore further. They learned too that working with someone else may help them achieve success more quickly and that arguing over who should carry something back is an unproductive use of time. As the clothing was collected and hung on the washing line we had discussed as the best way to show Busby we were finding it, we spent time creating patterns and counting in both English and French before exploring some of the home languages of the class.

142 Appendices

After this initial structured activity, I gave the children lots of free time to explore and learn. Most of the children chose to continue to use Busby as part of their play with many trying different ways to find him, or at least signs of his occupancy. I provided the children with equipment to use as they saw fit, e.g. magnifying glasses, binoculars, tarpaulins and rope. We observed children searching for Busby using binoculars, creating hides to watch for him, phoning Busby and even measuring areas to decide if they were big enough for the bear to use.

During the school week, Mrs Johnston continued to use Busby as a stimulus for classroom learning: the children wanted to write to Busby to tell him they had found his clothes and that he could collect them from the school. This showed just how invested in the whole idea of Busby this class had become and is testament to the collaboration between me as Forest School leader and their class teacher, as well as the accessibility of the Storyline approach.

Week 2

I wanted to continue to use the book and the ideas within the text to encourage the children in their play and to pick up and develop the ideas they had suggested in their plenary discussions from Week 1. The children were actively looking for Busby as we walked up the hill with many 'successful' sightings. They were keen to predict the content of this week's letter and had already expressed disappointment at Busby's apparent lack of gratitude for previous help they had given, as well as his poor handwriting.

This week, the letter thanked the children for their help (there was an audible sigh of satisfaction from our children) and a request for further help for his friend Mouse. Mouse was keen to spend time in the woods and requested holiday homes to be built to give him a choice of places to stay. Again, the purpose was to inspire collaborative and imaginative play and learning and to encourage adventure and exploration of their surroundings. This time, I was including *'appreciation of each others' qualities and contribution to the task'* as we reviewed everyone's home as part of the on-site plenary.

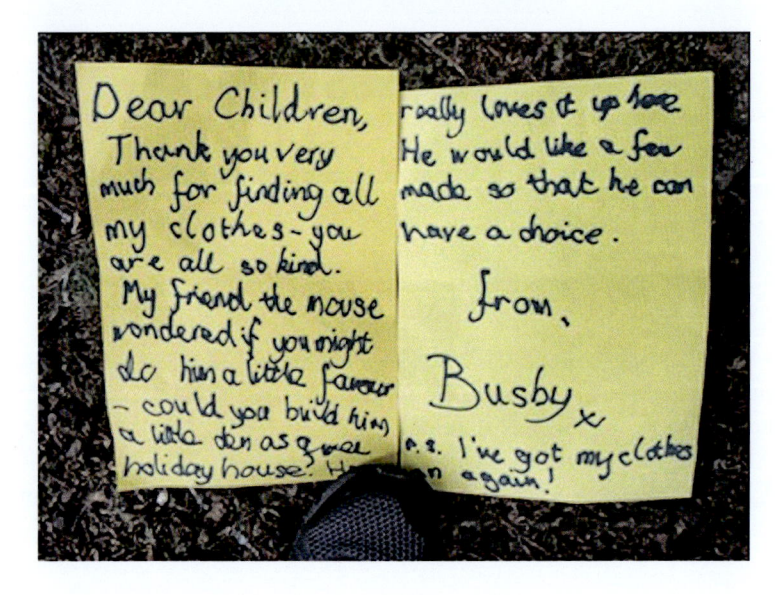

In Forest School children may choose who to partner up with for activities and there is always a fluidity within groupings and pairs and the option to work alone if desired. Some children are group butterflies and spend a short time in several groups, whilst others will remain on task with the same people throughout. It is very interesting to hear from the children in the plenary to see who claims ownership for which tasks completed and who might then need encouragement next time to show more resilience and sticking power. Mrs Johnston and I noted how children worked together in unlikely pairings: they begin to recognise that out in the woods different classmates may shine and appreciation of new skills and abilities becomes apparent.

Again, language work in class over the following week was inspired by the storyline unfolding in the woods. Den-building instructions were prepared.

Week 3

This week I wanted to add in the experience of *'keeping oneself safe when using larger-scale equipment,'* e.g. branches, rope and tarpaulins. These had all been available in previous weeks but had been used by a small number of children only. Now I wanted to see how the whole class might make use of them within the initial, structured task. At St Peter's we have a programme of Loose Parts Play two days each week in the playground, so the children are not unfamiliar with the use of larger-scale equipment, but the woodland is quite different from the concrete playground space.

Now that we had established the veracity of the envelopes and that these were safe for us to handle, this week's letter did not appear until we were actually on site. I made sure I completed the site risk assessment on my own rather than with a small group of children, as usual, to make sure I could set up the envelope tied round the tree. Much speculation and prediction had been discussed as we walked to our wood, particularly as no letter had been delivered to the school. The children were clearly still invested in the storyline and wanted Busby to continue to be part of their Forest School experience.

The children were delighted to find a new letter, and were intrigued to think it had been left for them on site. In the letter, the Friendly Ogre requested dens be built for him with enough space for everyone from the story to fit in. Quite a different prospect from the miniature homes built the previous week and requiring much more co-operation and experimentation. Children had to make use of the learning they had been developing through their STEM enquiries and problem-solving skills. Again, our observations showed great engagement from almost all the children, with one or two still needing encouragement to become actively involved. What was interesting was the level of discussion between the children about what to do and how, and how much Busby and the Ogre still featured in their conversations. The characters from their book were still foremost in their minds: they truly were building dens for the Ogre. One group chose to build close to their mouse house from the previous week to allow them to 'visit' each other, whilst another group built a new mouse house within their larger den because Mouse had "probably made new friends too." The building of these larger-scale dens encouraged the natural leaders to come to the fore.

Week 4

This was our last session. My scheduled task included an introduction to fire-building, in this instance making use of a storm kettle.

Busby left his final instructions in a bag with some raspberries to eat and the makings of hot chocolate for everyone. In his letter he thanked everyone for their help and friendship and explained that he had to move on to explore new woodland and make new friends with other schools, particularly as our woods were no longer very appealing to him. Our site had unfortunately been damaged by members of the public who had chosen to build fires irresponsibly and not clear up afterwards. The fires had damaged trees and left them in an awful state. The children had been shocked in the previous weeks to find the area treated in this way. One of the responsibilities of Forest School is to educate children in how to have fires responsibly and to leave the area unscarred once we are finished. Busby charged us to do this when we used the storm kettle to boil water for our drinks.

Using Busby and our storyline like this could have backfired: the end goal should be an uplifting moment; a culmination of the learning which has taken place – a celebration, if you will. The devastation of our site was significant, and the children needed to be offered an outlet to be able to express their anger and distress without it becoming a pity-fest. I wanted the children to feel rightly outraged but to take positive action and appreciate that they were responsible citizens who knew how to manage their fun in the woods.

We achieved this through sensitive handling of the vandalism issue and discussion and debate both on site and back in class. The children have already made plans to find ways to improve the site when next they visit. Busby and his friends helped them to develop a love and pride in their learning space in the woods which we will build on over the coming years.

Clearly there are many aspects to our Forest School adventures which I have not detailed here as they are not entirely relevant to the Storyline approach. However, one thing I do wish to stress: you do not have to be a Forest School leader to take your class on outdoor learning adventures, but please make sure you have relevant risk assessments in place. Storyline fits in so well with the outdoors I would encourage everyone to consider how they might incorporate this into their own planning. Provided you plan for the unexpected and hold the line in terms of the main aspects of learning you wish to achieve, taking your class outdoors is a most rewarding experience, particularly if you bring it back into class to develop there too.

Appendix 9

Practitioner example: Our Railway

A storyline using the conventions of the Visitor and the Challenge

In this storyline a visitor comes to see the class.

The visitor tells them that she has recently moved to the area and is interested in old railways. She is hoping to hold an exhibition based on the local railway lines and stations no longer in use, but needs help with setting it up.

She asks the class if they would help her and provides them with a 'design specification' for the task (see below).

Here are some of the things I will need for the exhibition:

1. Maps of the area from the days that the railways were running
2. Up-to-date maps to show what has happened
3. Old photographs from your parents, grandparents or local newspapers or online
4. Information about the jobs people did on the railways and in support of them. I am especially interested in the time when the railway was doing well, so you could research around the 1930 to 1960 period
5. Something about what life would have been like for adults and for children then
6. Any old posters, leaflets or adverts to do with the railways
7. Some models for visitors to look at: a model of the station, of the railway cottages and the old school, for example
8. Anything about local landmarks that we had then and some that still exist
9. Something about how the land is used now – cycle ways, etc.
10. Something about the wildlife that can now flourish along the routes of the old railways

---

The class would then be left with the teacher to plan how they would help our visitor.

The proposed exhibition would be planned with groups of children responsible for different aspects of the material needed to tell the story of the old railway.

It might be that the device of a 'family' and a 'street' is used to tell the tale, or the project could simply be based on what they might expect to see at a museum.

The class might visit a local museum to get ideas regarding their task.

The learning would cover outcomes in History, Literacy and Technology.

The celebration would of course be the exhibition and a return visit from the visitor.

The assessment evidence would be notes on the process as well as the obvious 'product' of the exhibition itself.

Parents, grandparents and members of the community could be involved in the research and the provision of artefacts and, of course, could provide the audience for the exhibition of what the children learn through this storyline.

Appendix 10

Practitioner example: the Middle Ages (the Challenge)

For this storyline the class will have already been learning something about life in the Middle Ages and have some idea about when this was and what life was like. The idea of the challenge is to try to contextualise this learning and to provide a vehicle for them to share what they know. It will involve them learning more things, of course, and once they are 'hooked in' they will also add elements from their own interest to enhance the basic idea.

At a suitable point in the project the teacher can present them with the following challenge.

Three weeks from now we are going to have a Middle Ages ball.
Everything about this ball should be just as it was in the Middle Ages:

- The guests will wear clothes similar to what they had in the Middle Ages.
- The food will be similar to what they had in the Middle Ages.
- The entertainment will be just like what they had in the Middle Ages.
- There will also be jesters, dancing and singing.
- During the ball there will be a presentation to show some of the things you have learned about the life, work and entertainment of the Middle Ages.

Everyone will have a role in preparation for the ball and also something to do during the great occasion.

Having been presented with this challenge, the class will consider what has to be done and think about the best way to be ready for the big day.

In terms of learning they will cover a lot of social skills, such as discussion, teamwork, problem solving, co-operation and negotiation. They will learn a good deal of history as well as research skills: reading for information, note taking, report writing and presenting information.

In terms of literacy they will create posters, fact files and letters to support their role as well as creating invitations for the ball itself.

In terms of the expressive arts there will be opportunities for drama, dance, singing and artwork.

Presenting this as a challenge to the class as a whole means there will be a lot of group and collaborative work. Pupils will be given jobs and responsibilities such as resource manager, script editor, quality controller and director.

The assessment evidence will be through observation of the process and also through the written work presented. It will also be through the presentation of information at some point during the ball.

The challenge should provide motivation, an audience and a purpose for learning all about life in the Middle Ages.

Appendix 11

Practitioner example: Egypt
A storyline using the conventions of the Visitor and the Letter

This storyline was created by a group of student teachers and designed for 8- to 10-year-old pupils.

The learning

Curricular area	Details	Assessment evidence
Literacy	Listening and talking, biographies, writing diaries, a newspaper report and a poster	Diary entries Biographies Newspaper report Poster
Social Studies	Learning about people from another time and place	Researching skills Note-taking Report writing Drama content
Drama	Hot-seating, conscience alley and thought-tapping	Use conventions with confidence "We are learning to express thoughts, feelings and ideas"

The hook

The classroom door is decorated to look like the entrance to a pyramid. The teacher is dressed as one of the Pharaoh's officials.

Once the children are in and seated, the official opens a scroll, which is a message from the Pharaoh that says, "I don't think everyone in my kingdom is working hard enough. I want you each to tell me who you are, who is in your family, and what your jobs are."

Lesson 1

In this first lesson the class will go on to discuss pyramids and the Egyptians and begin to complete a KWL grid showing what they already know and what they want to know and how they might find it out. This will form part of an ongoing wall display.

Lesson 2

Once the children are in and seated, the official opens a scroll, which is a message from the Pharaoh that tells them everything that the Pharaoh has done that day and ends with: "I want to know all about you and your lives!"

Following on from this the class will build on their research from Lesson 1 and begin to form biographies for their characters. Templates will be used to create characters for the display.

In order to create a mixture of family types each pupil will roll a dice to determine what their job is. This will prompt the need for further research and the recording of their findings.

Lesson 3

The groups will research and make models of their homes for a table 'street' display.

Lesson 4

Pharaoh's official comes with a message saying that the Pharaoh still doesn't think the children are working hard enough, so he wants an account of their day/week: "What is the daily life of your family? Create a diary of your day/week."

Lesson 5

The Pharaoh's official comes to proclaim that some of the children have been sold as slaves to noblemen.

Then hold a group discussion about how the slaves feel, how the nobles feel, how the other families feel. Do drama work on how this would look. Use 'thought tapping' and 'conscience alley' conventions to show how the characters feel. Take 'still pictures' for the wall display (these will be annotated afterwards).

Lesson 6

The Pharaoh's official says that one of the noblemen has died in an accident at work.

The groups are to suggest what this may have been. Each group is to produce a newspaper article about what happened.

Lesson 7

The class are asked to design and make a pyramid and research what to do in order to organise the mummification process.

Lesson 8

There is to be a party to celebrate the life of the deceased nobleman. The groups each have a job to do to prepare for the party.

Groups work on the food, clothing, decorations and entertainment in preparation for the big party.

Lesson 9

After a short ceremony to put the mummy in the tomb and seal the pyramid, the party takes place.

Lesson 10

The class plan an assembly to show the rest of the school what they have learned about the Egyptians through their Storyline experience.

The Pharoah is invited and is very impressed!

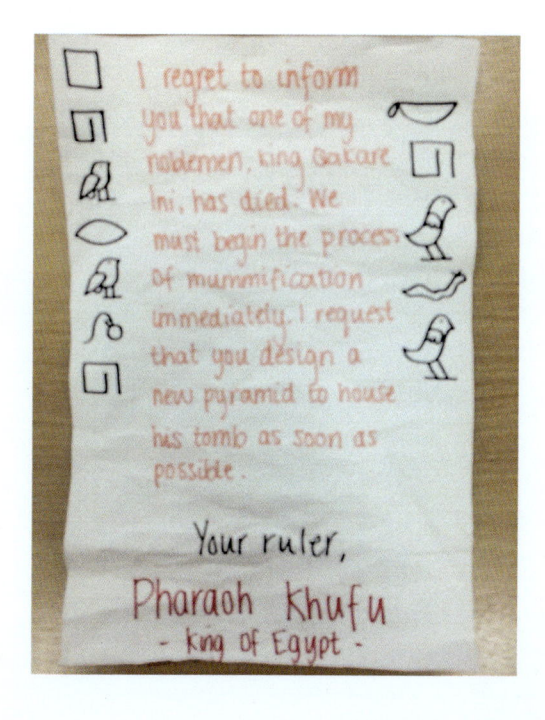

Appendix 12

Practitioner example: Wind Farm

A storyline using the conventions of the Visitor and the Letter

Synopsis

In this storyline the class will imagine they are part of a fictional community in the present-day Scottish Highlands. They will all have jobs and live in a rural village.

Once a sense of 'ordinary life' has been established a letter will arrive telling them of a proposal to build a huge wind farm nearby. They have to consider the impact this will have on them, their lives and their occupations. The impact on wildlife is also considered.

An expert is invited in to discuss this plan and so they must research as much information as they can in preparation for this event.

Their work is assembled into PowerPoint presentation to share when the visitor comes to visit them.

During the visit there is a debate and later a vote taken on whether or not the wind farm should go ahead.

The learning

Overall learning intentions:

I can describe the benefits and disadvantages of wind farms

I can think about my own point of view, and present a coherent argument using both spoken and written persuasive language

I am willing to listen to other people's points of view and arguments

CfE Experiences and Outcomes:

I can describe the major characteristic features of Scotland's landscape. SOC 2-07a

By considering the type of text I am creating, I can select ideas and relevant information, organise these in an appropriate way for my purpose and use suitable vocabulary for my audience. LIT 2-26a

Lesson 1

Learning: listening and talking, research, note taking, presenting a factual text

In Lesson 1 we set the scene and show some video footage of a remote rural community in Scotland. Working in groups, children are asked to make a list of things that:

- are similar to those where they live;
- are different from those where they live;
- they like better in this rural community;
- they prefer in their own community.

They are then given the choice of poster, grid, narrative or PowerPoint to show what they know about their own community compared to the rural community that will feature in our storyline.

Lesson 2

Learning: Social Studies, learning about what it like to live somewhere very different
 The teacher will introduce them to a person who lives in the rural community:

> When I put on the shawl and hat you have to imagine that I am Agnes McDuff from the Highland village in our story. You can ask me any questions about the village, the folk who live there and some of the local legends and history.

Getting the class to interact with the teacher in a role enables them to learn more about what life might be like. It also gives the teacher the opportunity to develop some ownership for the class and some connection with the village.

> You all seem very nice people, so I think I can trust you. We are only a small village and we have room for a few extra families to help get all of the work done. Please look at the pictures on your desks and use the materials to make houses to add to the village display.

They are told that they are going to imagine that they live and work in this location. Templates will be used to create a street for a frieze, or old shoeboxes could be used to create a three-dimensional village.

Lesson 3

> **CfE Experiences and Outcomes:**
> By considering the type of text I am creating, I can select ideas and relevant information, organise these in an appropriate way for my purpose and use suitable vocabulary for my audience. LIT 2-26a
> I can convey information, describe events, explain processes or combine ideas in different ways. LIT 2-28a

Next the children are divided into family groups and each given the chance to draw an occupation out of a hat. Then they must research all about the job they will be doing. These will be presented as pieces of writing – a diary, biography or written narrative.

Some occupations to consider:

---

1 Fisherman/woman
2 Baker
3 Hotel/pub worker
4 Shop manager
5 Post office worker
6 Teacher
7 Farmer
8 Environmental workers (RSPCA/RSPCB workers)

Lesson 4

Learning: listening and talking, writing a persuasive letter

Incident

The children arrive in the classroom to find a letter on their display. The letter tells them that they may need to leave their village so that a wind farm can be built nearby.

As the class react to this news the teacher will ask them what they might do about this.

A protest letter would then be compiled by each family group to send to the developer.

Lesson 5

Learning: listening and talking, research, note taking, presenting a factual text.

A visitor

In the next lesson the teacher will announce that in response to their letters of protest she has invited an expert from the wind farm to come in and talk to them.

As the expert will be knowledgeable about this subject it is important that the children have some knowledge too. Perhaps they could visit a wind farm.

Using a carousel approach the children will be asked, "What do you already know?", "What do you need to know?" and "How will you find out?"

As a result of this they will work in groups to research the pros and cons of a wind farm for their area.

Learning focus: research about wind farms. What do they do? What are they like? Why do we need them? Where do they need to be? Is there somewhere else, other than our village, that they could go?

In order to influence the visitor when they come, the class are asked to consider the impact the wind farm will have on their community. Each family has to present an account of the benefits and disadvantages for them. This will be done in the form of a PowerPoint presentation given by the class (as a practice) prior to presenting this to the visitor.

Learning focus: decide how wind farms would affect the family occupations – begin to devise arguments for the pros and cons of wind farms.

> **CfE Experiences and Outcomes:**
>
> I can persuade, argue, explore issues or express an opinion using relevant supporting detail and/or evidence. LIT 2-29a
>
> I can use evidence selectively to research current social, political or economic issues. SOC 2-15a
>
> I can consider the advantages and disadvantages of a proposed land use development and discuss the impact this may have on the community. SOC 2-08b

Children will discuss the impact of the wind farm on their family groups and on the local and wider communities – they will need to decide if their family is for or against the wind farm.

> **CfE Experience and Outcome:**
>
> I can select ideas and relevant information, organise these in an appropriate way for my purpose and use suitable vocabulary for my audience. LIT 2-06a

Children can create a poster or leaflet to display how their family feels about the proposed wind farm. This piece of work should provide evidence of what they have learned so far from their research, their wind farm visit and the discussion with the expert.

Lesson 6

> **CfE Experiences and Outcomes:**
>
> I can consider the advantages and disadvantages of a proposed land use development and discuss the impact this may have on the community. SOC 2-08b
>
> I can describe the main features of a democracy and discuss the rights and responsibilities of citizens in Scotland. SOC 2-17a
>
> I can convey information, describe events or processes, share my opinions or persuade my reader in different ways. LIT 1-28a/LIT 1-29a

Go over the rules and format of a debate and prepare the class for their roles in this.

Each family will present their feelings and evidence and try to persuade the others as to their point of view.

The visitor will arrive and present a persuasive case for building the wind farm in their community.

The teacher, in the role of Agnes, will put forward some opposing views about how the wind farm might adversely affect their community.

Each family will each present their views on the wind farm proposal.

After everyone has done their presentation there will be a vote to decide whether the wind farm can go ahead or not.

This debate will provide another opportunity to assess the knowledge, understanding and attitudes of the class as well as their skills in terms of debating, presenting information and accepting the different views of others.

At the end of the debate there might be a celebration in the 'village hall.'

Appendix 13

Practitioner example: New Neighbours and Refugees (the Street)

For this example, we will use the Storyline planning format that you have seen elsewhere in this book.

Plan

1	Choose the context	How would you react if a new/strange/annoying neighbour moved into your street?
2	Decide on the learning *focus*	Health and Wellbeing and new neighbours What it is to be a family/ neighbour
3	Decide on the *kind* of storyline	Using a family and a street to immerse the class in the learning
4	Decide on a *way in* (the hook)	Creating a 'modern' family in a present-day street
5	Think about the *progression through the topic*: Who? When? Where?	They will create families and homes We will explore what 'normal life' might be for these people We will explore some positive relationships within the family and the street Then new neighbours will arrive and there will be some tension and conflict to be resolved
6	Focus *on the learning*, the key questions, the skills, knowledge and attitudes, and how you might assess the learning	What do we mean by 'family'? How do families get on? How do they resolve conflict and cope with problems? What is it to be a good neighbour? How can we get along with our neighbours? What is diversity? How can we better understand people who are different from us?
7	Plan for *progress through* the topic: normal life, its tasks, celebrations, rituals and routines	Create the family Create our street Normal life Something about us Relationships within the family Relationships with others in the street Our reaction to the new neighbours What can we do? A party or joint venture with/for them
8	Plan the *special event*, celebration, turning point or climax to end the narrative	Getting to know the new neighbours A party or joint venture with/for them
9	Think about how you will facilitate the *reflection and evaluation* of the story and the learning that has taken place	Retelling the story as a blog and a video

Appendix 13 157

10 Consider what *evidence* you might have at the end of the topic to show the learning that has taken place
- Biographies
- Notes on the oral stories
- Writing: a day in my life
- My first impression of the new neighbours
- Ideas for resolving conflict
- Invitation to get to know them
- Discussion regarding transferrable skills when you come across diversity: what is diversity? How can we better understand people who are different from us?

Progression through the topic

In this topic, we begin by using the conventions of the family and the Street (see Chapter 5).

1 We are going to pretend that each group is a family living in this town in this year.
2 Each member of your group will be a person in this family. Begin by discussing who you want to be and what you feel a good family would look like.

Discussion

At this point the children can have a number of responses: they might go for an 'ideal family,' perhaps one they themselves never had, or they might go for the 'unusual,' with something different from the conventional mum, dad and two children. For this topic it really does not matter but it is better if they have to be of an age between 7 and 70 in order to allow scope for writing and drama tasks.

3 You need now to create your character using the stencil provided.	Creating characters
4 Each character will be stuck onto a family portrait sheet.	
5 Next you need somewhere to live. Using the materials provided create your family home. These will be added to the display on the wall.	Creating homes

On the classroom wall, there will be space for each house. In the middle of the street there will be a space where the 'new neighbour' will later be added. I like to put a 'play park' here so the children will have a reaction later on when I take it away to build on!

6 Now that you have a family and a home I want to learn something about you. You are going to create a biography for your character. We want to know the following: Who are you? How old are you? What do you like/dislike? How do you spend your time? Do you work? Do you have any hobbies or talents? How do you get on with everyone in your family? Tell us about your house – what do you like/dislike about it?	Writing: biography
7 Now you are going to meet someone from another family in the street. Introduce yourself and ask them a few questions about themselves. You will get to do this three times, so you will have some friends in the street.	Listening and talking

Appendix 13 159

8 Today you are going to tell us all about 'normal life.' Listening and talking
   Imagined personal writing

   You will tell your partner about a typical day, from getting up until going to bed.
   Later we will write about this as a piece of imagined personal writing.

9 You may have noticed a change in our display today. Listening and talking

   Yes, there seems to be a 'For sale' sign on the land where we have the 'play park.'
   How do you feel about this?
   What do you think will be built there?
   What would you like to be built in our street?

At this point the story could go in any number of directions:

- The class might feel strongly about the park and want to protest.
- This can lead to them writing to the council, campaigning for the park to be left alone.
- They might decide that the street needs a shop or leisure centre. Again, this can lead to some rich discussion, negotiation, research and creative ideas.
- In this story, the land is sold and next time they come in they will see a new house in the street.

10	So, there is a new house, which means you will have new neighbours! In your family group share your understanding of the word 'neighbour.'	Mind map
11	Create a mind map showing what you think makes a 'good' neighbour.	Listening and talking
12	Let's create 'success criteria' for a good neighbour.	Writing/justifying
13	It is sometimes difficult to get to know new people. In our drama today we are going to share ideas and try out some strategies for meeting and getting to know new people.	Drama
14	Today you are going to meet the new neighbours: the McSweens. The new neighbours are quite lively. Dad is unemployed and likes to spend his spare time fixing cars in the front drive. Let's draw what Dad might look like.	Discuss/draw
	Mum likes to party and often comes home late at night singing loudly. Let's draw what Mum might look like.	Discuss/draw
	Sam has a skateboard and she likes to make ramps and jumps in the street to play with her gang. Draw Sam.	Discuss/draw
	Joe is a quiet boy who says very little and is often seen looking out of his bedroom window with a book in his hand. Draw Joe.	Discuss/draw
15	There is another person who lives in the house.	Writing
	This person is called Ash. Create this character. Decide what they look like. How old are they? Is it a boy or a girl? Tell us something about them.	
16	What do you think about the new family?	Discussion
	How will your character react to them?	
17	I have divided the class into pairs, 'A' and 'B.'	Drama
	Person A will be a person from the new family. Person B will be their character from the street family. Act out an interaction between these two characters. Swap roles and repeat.	
18	Now, in your family groups you have been divided so that one family will be 'themselves' from the street and the other will be the McSween family.	Drama
	Create an interaction between the two families. Swap roles and repeat.	
19	In our Drama lesson, we created an interaction between the two families. Today you are going to write the story of what happened and how it was resolved.	Imaginative writing
20	We need to bring our storyline to a close. Let's think up an event or celebration that will get the whole street together. Then we can plan a street party, create invitations and posters and organise roles for everyone. What will we need?	

At this point the class will decide on how to end the topic. Jobs can be delegated with different families responsible for food, entertainment, advertisements, etc.

After the party there will be a plenary lesson where we discuss:

- what we did;
- what we learned;
- how we learned;
- the evidence to show what we learned;
- the transferrable knowledge, skills and attitudes we have developed.

Adaptations of 'the New Neighbours'

If you want to have more of a focus on diversity you can adapt the plan at Point 16:

- You might introduce a family with some sort of disability.
- It might be a family with different religious beliefs.
- It could be refugees from another country.

In each of these scenarios the class will be aware of similarities and differences. They will have preconceived (often stereotyped) views already. They will need to do research, ask questions and think about tolerance and inclusion.

Refugees storyline (using the Scottish Curriculum for Excellence Experiences and Outcomes)

16 Refugees arrive in the new house. 　Who are they? What do they look like? 　Why are they here? 　In what ways are they like us? 　In what ways are they different?	Imaginative writing
17 Each group will be given a character from the refugee house to research. We need to know: 　• Their name, what they look like, why they are here. 　• What do they do? A list of similarities and differences to you.	

Learning:

- By comparing the lifestyle and culture of citizens in another country with those of Scotland, I can discuss the similarities and differences. SOC 2-16c
- Develop my understanding of my own values and beliefs. SOC 2-19a

At this point you might need to decide who the refugees are and where they are from. If you guide children to selected websites they will be able to learn that being different doesn't necessarily mean looking different. They might also learn that in order to understand someone who seems different you need to find out something about them.

You might support this by dressing up and being 'teacher in role' or letting them 'hot seat' you. You might invite a parent in to pretend to be one of the family there to answer questions.

18 You need to find out if the new neighbours have any different ways of living. Research clothes, food and religion and be ready to report back to the class.

Learning:

- Develop my understanding of my own values and beliefs. SOC 2-16C
- I am developing my understanding of how my own and other people's *beliefs and values* affect their actions. RME 2-09d

162   *Appendices*

Depending on the class and the culture of your school you might extend the learning into a debate.

19 The new family face a lot of challenges. Discuss these challenges and compare their lives to yours. How might we help the new family to settle in?	Social Studies Debate

Learning:

- Develop my understanding of my own values and beliefs. SOC 2-16c
- I am developing my understanding of how my own and other people's *beliefs and values* affect their actions. RME 2-09d
- I can discuss issues of the diversity of cultures, values and customs in our society. SOC 2-16c
- By comparing the lifestyle and culture of citizens in another country with those of Scotland, I can discuss the similarities and differences. SOC 2-16c
- I can gather and use information about forms of discrimination against people in societies and consider the impact this has on people's lives. SOC 2-16b

20 Our story needs a happy ending.
How can we end it so that everyone is happy?
What can we tell our audience about tolerance, difference and learning to get along together without discrimination and prejudice?

21 Your new neighbours have invited you to a celebration meal.
What will you/they wear?
What will you eat?
Find out what is needed in order to accept the invitation.
What can you tell them about Scotland?
Make a poster showing things that are similar/different between their life in (Syria) and your life in Scotland.

At this point the class may wish to invite in an audience – another class, parents or the whole school in assembly to share what they have learned.

Charting the learning (Scottish curriculum)

Below are some of the Curriculum for Excellence outcomes covered by this topic.

RME Outcomes

Developing an increased awareness and appreciation of the diversity of beliefs and values held by others
RME 2-09c

- I can explain why different people think that values such as honesty, respect, and compassion are important and I show respect for others

RME 2-09d

- I am developing my understanding of how my own and other people's beliefs and values affect their actions

Social Studies Outcomes

Learning in the social studies will enable me to:
SOC 2-16c

- Develop my understanding of my own values, beliefs and cultures and those of others

SOC 2-19a

- By comparing the lifestyle and culture of citizens in another country with those of Scotland, I can discuss the similarities and differences

Assessment evidence

- I can explain some of the customs and beliefs held by myself and others
- I can present some similarities and differences among cultures in Scottish society

Assessment evidence

- I can discuss issues of the diversity of cultures, values and customs in our society
- I can discuss the similarities and differences between my own family and one from another culture or religion

Appendix 14

Synopsis planning pro forma

Way in/introduction/hook

Progression through story

Concluding episode

Appendix 16

Storyline planning template

1 Choose the context	
2 Decide on the learning *focus*	
3 Decide on the *kind* of storyline	
4 Decide on a *way in* (the hook)	

5 Think about the *progression through the topic*:
 	
   Who?
 	
   When?
 	
   Where?	

6 Focus *on the learning*, the key questions, the skills, knowledge and attitudes and how you might assess the learning	
7 Plan for *progress through* the topic: normal life, its tasks, celebrations, rituals and routines	
8 Plan the *special event*, celebration, turning point or climax to end the narrative	
9 Think about how you will facilitate the *reflection and evaluation* of the story and the learning that has taken place	
10 Consider what *evidence* you might have at the end of the topic to show the learning that has taken place	

Appendix 17

WWII complete synopsis

Way in/introduction/hook

Read a passage from *The Machine Gunners* to set the scene of WWII in context.

Progression through story

Establish the families that live in the street in a city in WWII – focus on character descriptions, homes, occupations.

Find out about the difficulties of normal daily life in WWII – the blackout, gas masks, rations, etc. Explore the impact on the characters.

Unusual event – more people are needed for the war effort and a family member is conscripted.

Turning point – an air raid. Houses destroyed. Area no longer safe for children. What will happen now?

Evacuation – where might the children be going? With whom might they be living? Stage the evacuation process – the journey, being chosen, meeting the new family.

Concluding episode

Settling in with a new family.

Writing a letter to parents to describe new surroundings.

Appendix 18

WWII complete plan

Way in/introduction/hook	Read a passage from *The Machine Gunners* setting the scene of WWII context: place and time.
Tell class we are going to pretend we are living at that time in that street.

Elements	Questions	Learning	CfE Outcomes & Experiences	Activities	Evidence/assessment

Place
Time
Characters
	Who is in your family, what do they do and what do they look like?	• Group work skills
		• Creating ownership and creating an identity for the topic
		• Sharing what we already know
		• Identifying what we do not know
			As I listen or watch, I am learning to make notes under given headings and use these to understand what I have listened to or watched and create new texts.
			LIT 1-05a
			I can compare aspects of people's daily lives in the past with my own by using historical evidence or the experience of recreating an historical setting.
			SOC 1-04a
				Back in time
				Group tasks:
				• 'Carousel' on life at that time
				  • What did they look like?
				  • What were houses like?
				  • How did they dress?
				  • What jobs did they do?
				• Then create your own family, draw, cut out for frieze
				• Create houses for street
				• Write 'family profiles'
					• Wall frieze
					• Family profiles
					• Carousel comments

Normal daily life	What are the difficulties of daily life?	• What we know and can find out about the rules needed for life at that time • How to evaluate persuasive text as a source of evidence • How to produce a poster to inform	I can find, select, sort and use information for a specific purpose. LIT 1-14a I understand that evidence varies in the extent to which it can be trusted and can use this in learning about the past. SOC 1-01a I can compare aspects of people's daily lives in the past with my own by using historical evidence or the experience of recreating an historical setting. SOC 1-04a	Letters pinned to doors, warning notes on frieze, i.e.: • Breaking the blackout rules • Losing gas mask • Getting new ration book • Dig for victory	Create a group poster about each of the notes/ messages
Unusual event	What is conscription?	Learning what conscription was, why it was needed and how it worked Write an imagined personal response (letter) What are 'reserved occupations'? Effect on women and workforce	I can describe and share my experiences and how they made me feel. ENG 1-30a I can use evidence to recreate the story of a place or individual of local historical interest. SOC 1-03a	More people needed for war effort, each family has a person called up Each family member writes a letter as a response to one person being called up; i.e. to complain to officials, to record feelings, to write to a relative	List jobs that needed to be done, create posters for them Letters written about how they feel about someone in family being called up

Turning point or decision	What if we are attacked?	Why civilians were bombed Why certain places were targeted How people protected themselves The reality of a night in a shelter How to write instructions	I can compare aspects of people's daily lives in the past with my own by using historical evidence or the experience of recreating an historical setting. SOC 1-04a I am learning to use my notes and other types of writing to help me understand information and ideas, explore problems, generate and develop ideas or create new text. LIT 1-25a	Air raid siren goes off. What does it mean? What will we do? • Gather ideas about how to protect ourselves • Design shelters • Research information • Create models or Anderson shelters • Street air raid shelter • Read passages about life in shelters • Writing instructions for when the siren goes off and/or for making a shelter	Instructions for when the siren goes off Instructions for making a shelter Models of shelters
	Where will we live now?	Learning about evacuation: Why? Where? When? How? Impact of?	I can compare aspects of people's daily lives in the past with my own by using historical evidence or the experience of recreating an historical setting. SOC 1-04a	One of the houses is destroyed by a bomb The school and street to be evacuated: • Discussing and listing what to take • Making labels • Looking at maps to see where children might be sent from your city	Lists Labels Map work
		Role-play, listening and talking outcomes: sharing thoughts, feelings	When I engage with others, I know when and how to listen, when to talk, how much to say, when to ask questions and how to respond with respect. LIT 1-02a	Read extracts about what it was like to be evacuated Stage the evacuation and 'being chosen' Meeting new characters of the host family	Record/video Observation of interactions in role
Resolution/ celebration		Writing imagined personal letter/account	I can describe and share my experiences and how they made me feel. ENG 1-30a	Setting in Write the letter that tells parents where you are living and what it is like	Letters

Appendix 19

Rainforest complete synopsis
The tropical rainforest

Way in/introduction/hook

The class will be split into groups and told that we are going to do a storyline project. They will create modern-day families.

Later their families will receive letters to say that they have won a competition to have a holiday on the fringes of the tropical rainforest.

They will need to research where the tropical rainforests are located, and some tourist information on the proposed holiday area.

Progression through story

Once the groups have done some preliminary research they will be told that they are going to the Amazon river basin area, where there is a tropical rainforest.

Unfortunately, their hotel is unfinished and they have to cut down some trees to create huts to stay in.

In class they will use 'found material' (sticks, twigs, vegetation, etc.) to make models of homes that might exist if they actually lived in the rainforest.

Once the families and homes are established and some of the research has been done, there will be a visit from an 'expert' to tell them about the threat to the rainforest. The visitor will be from Conservation International and will be cross that they cut down some of the forest!

She asks them what they know about the rainforest, and sets them a task of finding out specific information in time for a return visit. She asks them to research the deforestation problem and to come up with ideas to tackle this.

The visitor will then ask them to try to come up with ideas for a publicity campaign to raise awareness and funds to try to protect the rainforest.

Concluding episode

Work will be done on posters, leaflets and adverts, and a short drama will be filmed. Fundraising ideas will be shared, including information on fair trade.

A fundraising event will be planned, selling smoothies and healthy snack bars using fair-trade products.

Appendix 20

Rainforest complete plan

Way in/introduction/hook

> Groups will be modern-day families who win a holiday in the tropical rainforest. When they arrive their accommodation will be unfinished so they have to make homes using local materials. They cut down some trees and make huts to stay in.
>
> A representative from Conservation International comes to tell them off for cutting down the trees. He asks them what they know about the rainforest, and sets them a task of finding out specific information in time for a return visit. He asks them to research the deforestation problem and to come up with ideas to tackle this.

Elements	Questions	Activities	Evidence/assessment	English Curriculum	CfE Outcomes & Experiences
Place Time Characters	Who are you? Where is the tropical rainforest? Who lives there?	Create characters in families Make homes using 'found materials' Research 'life in the rainforest'	Posters, maps, information leaflets, fact files Create 'advert' for rainforest Rainforest products display Campaign project plan	**GEOGRAPHY** Identify the positions and significance of the rainforests. Ge2/1.1 Understand geographical similarities and differences between the UK and a region in North or South America. Ge2/1.2a Describe and understand key aspects of physical geography, and human geography, including: types of settlement and land use, economic activity including trade links. Ge2/1.3a Use maps, atlases, globes and digital/computer mapping to locate countries and describe features studied. Ge2/1.3b	**SOCIAL STUDIES** I can explain how the physical environment influences the ways in which people use land by comparing my local area with a contrasting area. SOC 2-13a By comparing the lifestyle and culture of citizens in another country with those of Scotland, I can discuss the similarities and differences. SOC 2-19a I can explain how the physical environment influences the ways in which people use land by comparing my local area with a contrasting area. SOC 2-13a I can consider the advantages and disadvantages of a proposed land use development and discuss the impact this may have on the community. SOC 2-08b
Normal daily life	What would it be like to live in the rainforest? What is happening to the rainforest now?	Research and present some information about the rainforest in response to the questions for the visitor			
Unusual event	What is deforestation? Why is it a problem? What can be done about it?	Present some information about what we get from the rainforest and reasons why we need to protect it Come up with a campaign and ideas to raise funds to protect it		**SCIENCE** Living things and their habitats: describe how living things are classified into broad groups. Sc6/2.1a	
Turning point or decision	How can we organise our own campaign to save the rainforests?	Organise a campaign: have managers, researchers, press officers, actors, etc. Plan a fundraising and information awareness event	Organisation and execution of roles in the campaign, evidence in the process and the product of this work Presentation of ideas and information Rainforest fundraising products and the justification for the fundraising campaign		**LANGUAGE** I can persuade, argue, explore issues or express an opinion using relevant supporting detail and/or evidence. LIT 2.29a

(continued)

(continued)

Elements	Questions	Activities	Evidence/assessment	English Curriculum	CfE Outcomes & Experiences
Celebration	How can we help to save the tropical rainforests?	Fundraising exhibition and fundraising sale of products	Presentation of ideas and information Rainforest fundraising products and the justification for the fundraising campaign	ENGLISH Building a varied and rich vocabulary and an increasing range of sentence structures, organising paragraphs around a theme in narratives, creating settings, characters and plot. En3/3.3b Read their own writing aloud, to a group or the whole class, using appropriate intonation and controlling the tone and volume so that the meaning is clear. En3/3.3e	When I engage with others I can respond in ways appropriate to my role. Show that I value others' contributions to use these to build on thinking. LIT 2.02a ART Inspired by a range of stimuli, I can express and communicate my ideas, thoughts and feelings through activities within art and design. EXA 2-05a DRAMA I can create, adapt and sustain different roles, experimenting with movement, expression and voice and using theatre arts technology. EXA 2-12a

Appendix 21

Deforestation example

By Jenny Bayliss (who was in her final placement at the time)

Classroom dynamics: some children struggled with positive behaviour choices and some with confidence issues, and some were low-ability writers. I wanted to 'ignite' their love for learning and felt that a drama-based topic could work for the classroom dynamics.

Lesson 1: context and pupil voice

Children were asked to discuss and write down things that they wanted to learn about within the topic of 'rainforests.'
  Many of the children wanted to learn about the animals and the type of people that lived there.
  They had some understanding of what deforestation was, but many wanted to further their learning about the topic.

Lessons 2-4: classroom rainforest development (storyline display)

Lessons focused on the development of the classroom display; a large rainforest was needed to set the scene for our storyline.
  A Henri Rousseau study inspired our rainforest foliage and creatures of the forest artwork.
  Rainforest layers helped us to understand the structure of the rainforest.
  These animals and foliage were added to the children's own classroom rainforest.

Lesson 5: research on rainforest tribes

The children studied the people who lived in the rainforest. They created their own tribe-families and these were added into their classroom rainforest. It was important that they developed an attachment to their tribes; this was to support the storyline's effect in the future.

Lessons 6 and 7: debating and persuasive texts

We completed some learning on the 'art of persuasion' and focused on the language needed to persuade others. In drama, we set up a debate-style activity where the children began to prepare for different roles. Key skills of remaining in character, using persuasive language and creating a reasoned argument were covered in the learning. We looked at the groups of people who would be 'stakeholders' of the rainforest; for example, tribesmen, loggers, a forestry commission and environmentalists. These became our characters for our debate session.

Lesson 8: the event, 'trouble in the rainforest'

Today we combined our learning into our storyline. We kept the children outside of their classroom until they were given permission to enter. When they entered they found:

Appendix 21 179

- Their classroom rainforest had been covered with 'Get out' signs and red tape.
- Fire (orange cellophane on the windows) was coming towards their part of the rainforest.
- The room was filled with smoke.
- The noises of chainsaws were in the background.
- Their forest was about to be cut down.

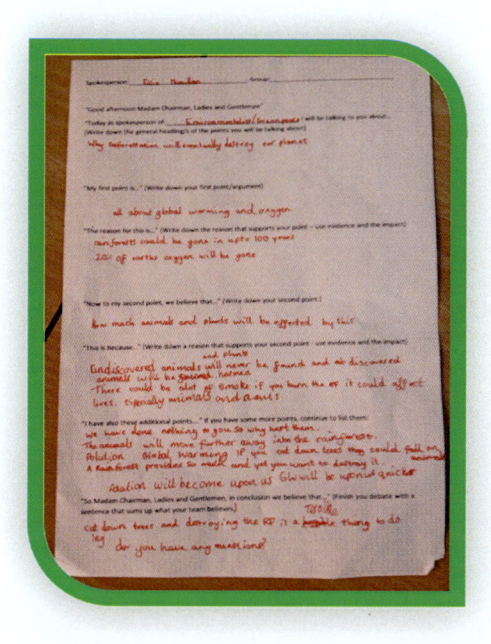

Children were given time to 'experience' the issue.

They were then asked to get into their stakeholder groups to discuss the situation. Notes were generated ready to bring forward to support their argument in a debate.

A debate was then set up, where they had to react – in character – to the danger to their classroom rainforest.

I played the role of the judge and each group had an opportunity to deliver their opinion on the deforestation of the classroom rainforest.

This was the end of my part in the storyline (my placement ended).

The feed-forward from the children is that they now wanted to delve deeper into the debate and play out the rest of the story . . . *What would happen to the rainforest?*

Appendix 22

Assessment pro forma

ASSESSMENT OF LEARNING: Date _____

Curricular area	
Learning intention	

	Success criteria	Assessment strategy
Needs more reinforcement 🔴		Formative Assessment used:
Generally achieved/ with support 🟡		• Thumbs up • Traffic lights • Two stars & wish • Peer comment
Achieved fully without support 🟢		• Peer marking • Self-marking • Show-me boards

NAME	TRAFFIC LIGHTS	COMMENTS

(continued)

(continued)

So what have I learned about my teaching?	So what have I learned about specific pupil progress/needs with this learning?

IMPLICATIONS: So what, **specifically**, will I do about this next time?
•   •   •

Appendix 23

Completed assessment grid

ASSESSMENT OF LEARNING: Date _____

Curricular area	English Language: Functional writing (in the style of a newspaper) Persuasive writing
Learning intention	I am writing in the style of a newspaper article I can select and use vocabulary to persuade and inform

Success criteria						Assessment strategy
Needs more reinforcement Generally achieved/with support Achieved fully without support	🔴 🟡 🟢	I can write in columns using a headline and a subheading	I can use 'wow' words to persuade the reader	I can use facts from WWII to inform and persuade	I can adopt the style of a newspaper report	Formative Assessment used: • Thumbs up • Traffic lights • Two stars & wish • Peer comment • Peer marking • Self-marking • Show-me boards

NAME	TRAFFIC LIGHTS				COMMENTS
Cara	🔴	🟡	🟢	🟡	Some good facts used but forgot the subheading and needs to work on using more 'wow' words
Brodie	🟢	🟢	🟢	🟢	Some excellent work in the style of a newspaper. Needs now to try to use more journalistic words
Daniel	🟡	🟡	🟢	🟡	Some good links to journalistic conventions but needs to include more facts
Eva	🟢	🔴	🔴	🔴	Although it is set out like a newspaper there needs to be more detail (didn't finish this!)

(continued)

184 Appendices

(continued)

Georgie		🟡	🟢	🟢	🟢	Forgot to write in columns until it was almost too late!
Hilda		🟢	🟢	🔴	🟡	A good attempt, but more detail needed, especially WWII-related information

So what have I learned about my teaching?	So what have I learned about specific pupil progress/ needs with this learning?
I need to check their understanding before I let them get started. Having a 'learning pit-stop' made a difference as it gave me a chance to remind some of them about writing in columns and using 'wow' words	Cara, Daniel, Eva and Georgie need support in processing the information. Next time I will get everyone to 'tell' their learning partner what they think they need to do for the task before they start working. Eva needs a scaffolding sheet to help her to focus and structure her work and to provide more detail.

IMPLICATIONS: So what, *specifically*, will I do about this next time?

- Have strategies for them to check their understanding of the task set
- Brainstorm facts to include with them and have this on the board
- Have a 'learning pit-stop' to share success and put everyone back on track

Appendix 24

Using templates

Whilst there will be some of your pupils who are excellent at drawing people, most will find this a struggle. Therefore, to be inclusive I like to provide a range of stencils to use as a starting point. Not only does this enable everyone to participate and be pleased with the results, it also ensures that the people are in proportion - with children generally being bigger than babies and smaller than adults, for example.

I provide a number of stencils to represent an adult male, child male, adult female and child female. If asked, I allow pupils to create smaller, younger family members as long as they are in proportion. Similarly, if they want to give their families a pet and I feel that this might enhance the story, it is also allowed.

If you were to do a storyline where the characters were not human – for example, Roald Dahl's *Fantastic Mr Fox* – then you could provide helpful stencils to scaffold the creation of the fox family instead.

I use black cards as the stencils as these are robust and hint at the creation of families that are not necessarily white. In modern storylines like 'New Neighbours' or 'Refugees,' children ask questions that challenge the stereotypical family composition. This means that you might get two dads, or two mums or a transgender child. It doesn't impair the storyline and in many ways it enhances the experience by celebrating diversity and enabling the participants to explore these issues from the safety of their characters. You might even consider including a stencil for someone in a wheelchair, again depending on the story.

Invariably we get twins! For over a decade I have done storyline families with primary school pupils, student teachers and visitors from China and the Netherlands, and the one consistent feature of the families is the desire to have twins!

Being a father of twins myself I had wondered if we humans had some desire or disposition towards the idea of being a twin, until I had a conversation with an eight-year-old recently. Referring to her classmate, she said, "Well, we are best friends in real life so I don't want to be just a brother or, worse, a mother to her in the story. If we are twins that's even better than being her best friend in real life!"

It is best to allow the participants to draw around the stencil and then to 'dress' it by cutting out hair, clothes, shoes, etc.

Later on, the character can be put on the family portrait sheet using Blu Tack. This allows you to move the characters around late on in the story. For example, if someone goes away to war, or dies or is lost, their character can be moved and only the outline will remain in the family portrait.

Having the characters made portable in this way also allows for them to be used as puppets in role-play situations, should the storyline permit this activity.

Building the houses can be done very simply too. I provide one rectangle as the house shape and another one with the corners cut off to be the roof. Children then have the opportunity to personalise the house with windows, a door, chimney, etc., depending on the era in which the house is to appear.

A completed one might look like this:

Alternatively, you might want to make the house three-dimensional, using a shoebox or half of a cereal box, or create something bespoke like the Scottish blackhouse below.

Of course, if you are doing a topic with something like aliens, anything goes and templates are an unnecessary obstacle to creativity!

Summary

It is clear then that providing a template can be inclusive, should not limit children's imagination and can enable them to 'live in someone else's shoes.' Often the child from the deprived home will create a 'perfect' and loving family as compensation. The 'only' child will create a sibling or twin. The child whose parents are not getting along may create a single-parent family to explore what that might feel like. The convention of creating a family is a very powerful one and having stencils to structure this means that any lack of skill in drawing people can be overcome and the real business of using your imagination to explore deeper issues can begin.

INDEX

accountability 18

active learning 14

Aliens: Alien story 119-120; Alien visitor 72-74, 94, 103, 105; Storyline in a day 111-116; writing frame 117-118

ambition 12

The Apprentice 69-70

Armitage, Ronda and David 74

Art and Design: Aliens 111, 120; assessment 104; curriculum developments 16, 18; curriculum planning 98-99; rainforests 85, 98, 176; The Street 42; Vikings 27

assessment 17, 21, 36, 83, 100, 101-105; Aliens 120; The Challenge 67, 69, 70; completed grid 183-184; curriculum planning 93; formative 11, 31, 76, 102, 106, 181, 183; Highland Clearances 130; The Middle Ages 148; national 18, 19; New Neighbours and Refugees 162; Our Railway 146; pro forma 181-182; rainforests 175-176; self and peer assessment 69, 107; strategies for 41; summative 10; systematic 106-107; The Visitor 76; WWII plan 170-171; *see also* evidence

attitudes 10, 11, 23, 41, 84, 98; The Challenge 70; Curriculum for Excellence 18; The Street 49

autonomy 13, 18, 19, 21, 70, 82

Bare Bear 140

Barnes, Jonathan 25, 26, 27

behaviourism 12

Bell, Steve 17

Berger 25

Black, Paul 31

the Blitz 41, 48, 126

Bloom's Taxonomy 24

brainstorming 42

Burns, Rabbie 77-78

Carr, David 13

celebrations 10-11, 35, 50, 83; Aliens 116, 120; assessment 104; The Challenge 67; choosing your Storyline approach 81, 90; Egypt 150-151; New Neighbours and Refugees 160, 162; Our Railway 145; rainforests 87, 176; The Street 49; The Visitor 71, 72, 77-78; Wind Farm 155; Wizard School 135; WWII plan 126, 171

The Challenge 66-70; assessment 101, 103, 105; choosing your Storyline approach 87, 88; curriculum planning 95; The Middle Ages 147-148

characters 6, 7-9; New Neighbours 158; rainforests 175, 178; The Street 44-45; templates 185-187; The Visitor 71-78; WWII plan 170

child-centred learning 16, 23

Clarke, Shirley 11, 31

classroom environment 24, 31

co-operative learning 31, 147

collaboration 4, 10, 30, 31; Forest School 142; interdisciplinary approach 28; The Middle Ages 147; The Social Studies 69; *see also* group work

communication 35

community 3, 4

conflicts 10

'connected' learning 32

Index

connections, making 5, 16, 24, 28, 29, 30
consulting the class 94-95, 105
context 4, 7, 81, 82
creativity 10
cross-curricular approach 19-20, 25, 27, 28
cross-disciplinary approach 26
cultural differences 161-162
curiosity 3, 4, 17, 72
curriculum 11, 13, 16-21, 23, 35; disciplines 14; flexibility 82; planning 92-99; teacher research 82-83
Curriculum for Excellence (CfE) 18-19, 24, 25, 30; interdisciplinary approach 28; New Neighbours and Refugees 161, 162; planning 42; rainforests 84, 175-176; Wind Farm 152, 153, 155; WWII plan 170-171

determination 11
Dharma Raja, B. William 26
didactic approach 13, 23, 29-30
difference, recognition of 24, 161; see also diversity
'dilemma letters' 63-64
direct teaching approach 13, 23, 29-30
disciplines 13, 14, 15, 20, 25, 28, 30
discovery 16, 23
diversity 161-162, 186; see also difference
Dragon's Den 66-69, 101; see also The Challenge
drama 10-11, 35, 90; Aliens 111; assessment 104; curriculum developments 16; Egypt 149; The Middle Ages 147; New Neighbours 160; rainforests 173, 176, 177-178; The Street 49
Dweck, Carol 11, 31

early years learning 14
Education Reform Act (1998) 17-18
Egypt 149-151
emotions 6, 54
employment 15
England 17-18, 19-20, 28, 84
English: assessment 106-107; curricular expectations 82; curriculum developments 18; rainforests 84, 85, 96, 176; see also Literacy; reading; writing
enthusiasm 4, 36, 37, 41, 65
epistemology 13
ethos 4, 19, 30, 31

evacuation 48-49, 126, 168, 171
evaluation 81, 90, 156
events/incidents 10, 50; choosing your Storyline approach 81; New Neighbours 156; rainforests 87, 175, 178-180; The Street 47; Wizard School 135; WWII plan 170
everyday life 10, 50; Aliens 114; choosing your Storyline approach 81, 89-90; New Neighbours 159; rainforests 87, 175; The Street 47; WWII plan 168, 170
evidence 36, 70, 81, 90, 98; curriculum planning 93, 94, 98; The Middle Ages 148; New Neighbours and Refugees 157, 162; Our Railway 146; planned learning 100; rainforests 175-176; The Visitor 76; WWII plan 170-171; see also assessment
experience, learning through 4

families 6, 7-9, 50, 101; Aliens 112-114; attitudes 84; Egypt 150; New Neighbours 157-158; rainforests 86, 88, 172; The Street 42-44; templates 185-187, 189; Wizard School 133-134; WWII plan 121, 168, 170
famous visitors 77-78
Fogarty, R. 29
Forest School 140-144
formative assessment 11, 31, 76, 102, 106, 181, 183
Freire, Paulo 24
fun 35, 62
future scenarios 51

Gardner's Multiple Intelligence approach 24
Geography: The Challenge 67; curricular expectations 82; curriculum developments 16, 17, 18, 20; rainforests 84, 85, 95-96, 175
Goodnight Mister Tom 42, 49
group work 13, 30, 31, 37; The Challenge 69; Forest School 143; interdisciplinary approach 28; The Middle Ages 147; Wind Farm 152; see also collaboration

Harkness, Sallie 9, 17
Hattie, John 11, 31
Health and Wellbeing 48, 63-64, 120
high school 15

Highland Clearances 127-132
Hirst, P.H. 25
History: The Challenge 67-69; curricular expectations 82; curriculum developments 16, 17, 18, 20; The Letter 62; The Middle Ages 147-148; Our Railway 145; The Street 50; The Visitor 77
holistic approach 16, 17
Holt, Deb 11, 32
homes 9, 50; Aliens 114; Egypt 150; New Neighbours 158; rainforests 86, 88, 172, 174; The Street 45-47; templates 187; Wizard School 134; WWII plan 121
hooks 42, 50, 81, 93; The Challenge 66; Egypt 149; New Neighbours 156; rainforests 88, 172, 174; The Visitor 73-74; WWII plan 169

imitation 12
incidental learning 85, 90, 93, 98-99, 101
inclusive approach 13
inspiration 93
integrated learning 26
intellectual quality 24
interdisciplinary approach 25-30, 107; The Challenge 67-69; classroom pedagogy 31; curriculum developments 16, 19, 20; curriculum planning 98-99; The Letter 62; transferrable learning 15-16
interest 12, 17, 41, 89

Jacobs, H.H. 26, 27
Jensenius, A.R. 26
Jeya Harish, H.G. 26
Johnson & Johnson 31
Jordanhill College of Education 17
Junior Dragon's Den 66-69

Khrishnakumar, R. 26
knowledge 49, 83, 85, 95, 98, 101
KWL grid 41-42, 98, 121, 149

learning 4, 10, 12-15, 21; The Challenge 70; choosing your Storyline approach 81, 82, 83-84, 89; 'connected' 32; control over 36-37, 69; curriculum developments 16-21; definition of 13; Egypt 149; emotional relationship with 3-4; with enthusiasm 65; evidence of 36, 90, 93, 94, 98; incidental 85, 90, 93, 98-99, 101; integrated 26; interdisciplinary 25-30; language of 105; learning how to learn 30, 32; New Neighbours and Refugees 156, 161-162; peer learning interactions 32; planned 100; plenaries 11; The Street 41; Wind Farm 152
The Letter 52-65; Aliens 119, 120; choosing your Storyline approach 87, 88; Egypt 149, 150; Forest School 140-144; Highland Clearances 129; Mary Queen of Scots 138-139; Wind Farm 152, 154
lifelong learning 11
The Lighthouse Keeper's Lunch 74-76, 104, 105
listening: Aliens 111; The Challenge 67; curriculum developments 16; Curriculum for Excellence 84; curriculum planning 97; Egypt 149; integrated learning 26; learning process 83; The Letter 62, 64, 65; New Neighbours 158-159, 160; plenaries 11; The Visitor 77; Wind Farm 152, 154
Literacy 14, 19, 23; Aliens 111; The Challenge 67, 69; curricular expectations 82; curriculum developments 17; Egypt 149; The Letter 62, 64; The Middle Ages 147; Our Railway 145; rainforests 84, 97, 98; The Street 42, 48, 50; The Visitor 77; *see also* English; listening; reading; talking; writing

The Machine Gunners 42, 168, 169
maps 104, 105
Mary Queen of Scots 137-139
Maths 17, 18, 120
Meeth, L.R. 26
mental health 63-64
metacognition 11, 32, 90, 105
The Middle Ages 104, 147-148
middle primary learning 14-15
Miller, A. 26
mind maps 49, 54, 119, 160
mindset 11, 31
models 103-104, 121-123, 150, 153, 172, 188
modes of enquiry 13, 14
Moss, Miriam 140
motivation 12, 28, 97
multi-disciplinary approach 26

Multiple Intelligence approach 24
narrative 3, 5-6, 17, 20-21

National Curriculum 17-18, 19-20, 30, 84, 175-176
negotiating skills 11, 35, 83, 147
New Neighbours and Refugees 156-162, 186
newspapers 50, 106-107, 138-139
numeracy 14, 23; *see also* Maths

observation 41, 70, 83, 93, 106, 148
Our Railway 145-146
outdoor learning 4, 140-144
The Owl Who Was Afraid of the Dark 52-63, 64, 103
ownership 6, 13, 30, 31, 50, 93; The Challenge 70; curriculum planning 95, 98

passion 3, 4, 37, 62, 72, 94, 95
Paterson, Lindsay 29-30
patterns 5
pedagogy 13, 30, 31, 35; *see also* 'Productive Pedagogy'
peer assessment 69, 107
peer learning interactions 32
pendulum theory 21
Piaget, J. 26
planning 42, 92-99; choosing your Storyline approach 81-91; New Neighbours 156; planned learning 100; pro forma 163-164, 165; rainforest complete plan 174-176; template 166-167; World War II complete plan 169-171
play 4, 14, 16, 23
plenaries 11, 136, 160
Plowden Report (1967) 17, 23
poetry 77, 103
positive mental health 63-64
'potpourri' problem 27, 70
presentations 10-11; The Challenge 67, 68, 69, 101; The Middle Ages 148; The Street 50; Wind Farm 152, 154-155
'Primary Education in Scotland 1965' (Primary Memorandum) 16, 23, 31
problem solving 10, 13, 35; early years learning 14; learning process 83; The Middle Ages 147; The Visitor 74-76
'Productive Pedagogy' 24-25, 30

progression 81, 83, 89, 156, 157-158, 168, 172
progressive education 23
project reviews 49, 50

rainforests 82, 84-91; assessment 103, 105; complete plan 174-176; complete synopsis 172-173; curriculum planning 95-97; deforestation example 177-180; incidental learning 98-99, 101
reading: curriculum developments 16; curriculum planning 97; integrated learning 26; The Letter 62, 65; plenaries 11; Storyline approach 35; Vikings 27
reflection 81, 90, 156
Refugees 161-162, 186
relationships 4
relevance 24
Rendell, Fred 17
research: Aliens 116; The Challenge 67, 68; Egypt 150; everyday life 89; The Letter 58, 62; The Middle Ages 147; plenaries 11; rainforests 177; The Street 47; teacher 82-83; Wind Farm 152, 154
resilience 11, 63, 143
Resnick, L. 28-29
responses 10, 12
reviews 49, 50
rewards 12
RME: Aliens 120; New Neighbours and Refugees 162; The Street 42, 48; Vikings 27

scaffolding 54, 64, 89, 186
Science: Aliens 120; curricular expectations 82; curriculum developments 16; The Letter 62; modes of enquiry 14; National Curriculum 18; rainforests 84, 85, 96, 175
Scotland 17, 18-19, 21, 84, 94; curricular guidance 82; interdisciplinary approach 28; 'Primary Education in Scotland 1965' 16, 23, 31; Scottish Storyline approach 17, 30; *see also* Curriculum for Excellence
self-assessment 69, 107
self-regulation 24
senses 12
social skills 62, 69, 83, 147
Social Studies: The Challenge 66, 69; curricular expectations 82; Curriculum for Excellence 84; curriculum planning 97-98; Egypt 149;

The Letter 62; New Neighbours and Refugees 162; rainforests 97, 98, 175; The Street 42, 48
socially supportive classroom environment 24
Socratic Questioning of Thought 24
software 73
stencils 185-189
Storyline approach 5-12, 21, 32, 34-38; choosing your 81-91; curriculum planning 92-99; learning and assessment 100-108; Scottish Storyline approach 17, 30; theoretical links 31-32
The Street 6, 41-51; choosing your Storyline approach 86-87, 88; Highland Clearances 127-132; New Neighbours and Refugees 156-162; Wizard School 133-136
subjects 13; *see also* disciplines
success criteria 36, 86, 101-102, 105, 106-107, 181, 183
summative assessment 10
suspension of disbelief 4, 65, 72, 77

talking: Aliens 111; The Challenge 67; curriculum developments 16; Curriculum for Excellence 84; curriculum planning 97; Egypt 149; integrated learning 26; learning process 83; The Letter 62, 64, 65; New Neighbours 158-159, 160; plenaries 11; The Visitor 77; Wind Farm 152, 154
Tarrant, Peter 11, 32
teachers 3, 4, 10; control over learning 36-37, 69; curriculum developments 16, 17, 18, 21, 23; feedback from 36; key assessment questions 93; planning 42; teacher research 82-83
teamwork 13, 35, 69, 147
Technology: Aliens 120; The Challenge 67-69; curriculum developments 18; incidental learning 101; Our Railway 145; Vikings 27

templates 185-189
Thaiss, Christopher 28
thematic learning 26
theoretical links 31-32
topic headings 94
traffic light system 102, 106-107, 183-184
transdisciplinary approach 26
transferrable learning 14, 15, 16
trust 3, 4

university 15
upper primary learning 15, 93
video 68-69, 73, 93, 104, 105

Vikings 27-28, 50, 94, 103, 104
visible learning 11, 31, 32, 105
The Visitor 71-78; assessment 103, 105; choosing your Storyline approach 87-88; curriculum planning 94; Egypt 149; Mary Queen of Scots 138-139; Our Railway 145-146; rainforests 172, 174; Wind Farm 152, 153, 154-155
Vygotsky, L. 31

ways of knowing 13
When Hitler Stole Pink Rabbit 42
William, Dylan 31
Wind Farm 152-155
Wizard School 133-136
World War II 3-4, 65, 121-126; assessment 101, 103, 104, 105; complete plan 169-171; complete synopsis 168; The Street 41-51
writing: Aliens 111, 114-116, 117-118; assessment 103, 106-107; curriculum developments 16; curriculum planning 97; Egypt 149; evidence 93; integrated learning 26; The Letter 52-65; New Neighbours and Refugees 158-159, 160, 161; plenaries 11; poetry 77; rainforests 85, 96; The Street 49, 50; Wind Farm 153